INSIGHT POCKET GUIDES

New Orleans

D1262096

APA PUBLICATIONS

Part of the Langenscheidt Publishing Group

L

New Orleans

1 mile/ 1,6 km

Lake Pontchartrain

Southern Yacht Club

WEST END

Lake Shore Dr.

SPANISH FORT

Lake Shore Dr.

Kiefer UNO Lakefront Arena

University of New Orleans East Campus

WEST END PARK

Mardi Gras Fountain

Elysian

Franklin Ave.

PONTCHARTRAIN PARK

Press Dr.

University of New Orleans Main Campus

Paris Ave.

Robert E. Lee Blvd.

Robert E. Lee Blvd.

Fields Rd.

Orpheum St.

Fleur de Lis Dr.

West End Blvd.

Canal Blvd.

Argonne Blvd.

VISTA PARK

Prentiss Ave.

Prentiss Ave.

Carroll Canal

Ursuline St.

LAKEVIEW

Harrison Ave.

CITY PARK

OAK PARK

MIRABEAU GARDENS

Mirabeau Ave.

Mirabeau Ave.

Mirabeau Ave.

GENTILLY TERRACE

Press Ave.

BONNABEL PLACE

Veterans Mem. Hwy.

Toulouse St.

Orleans Outfall Canal

Bayou St. John

St. Bernard Ave.

Paris Ave.

EDGEWOOD PARK

Gentilly Blvd.

Chef Menteur Hwy.

EDGEWOOD

Dillard University

Franklin Ave.

Delgado Jr. Community College

Storyland

Tod Gormley Stadium

Museum of Art (NOMA)

FAIR GROUNDS RACETRACK

Gentilly Blvd.

North Broad Ave.

Hope St.

Hope St.

Almonaster Ave.

Franklin Ave.

METAIRIE CEMETERY

GREENWOOD CEMETERY

City Park Ave.

Dueling Oaks

Esplanade Ave.

Metairie Rd.

Metairie Rd.

Longue Vue House and Gardens

Canal Street

Canal Blvd.

Orleans Ave.

Carrollton Ave.

North Claiborne Ave.

North Robertson St.

St. Bernard Ave.

St. Claude Ave.

Airline Hwy.

MID CITY

Tulane Ave.

North Broad Ave.

North Orleans Ave.

Canal Street

Theatre of the Performing Arts

Esplanade Ave.

Franklin Ave.

Earhart Blvd.

South Claiborne Ave.

Xavier University

Pontchartrain Expwy.

South Broad Ave.

LOUIS ARMSTRONG PARK

St. Louis Cathedral

Old US Mint

CARROLLTON

Carrollton Station Streetcar Barn

Washington Ave.

Earhart Blvd.

ST. LOUIS CEMETERY NO. 1

FRENCH QUARTER

Jackson Square

Patterson Rd.

ALGIERS POINT

St. Charles Ave.

Broadway

Tulane Stadium

BROADMOOR

Napoleon Ave.

Toledano St.

South Claiborne Ave.

Jackson Ave.

Duncan Plaza

City Hall

Civic Center

New Orleans Centre

Lousiana Superdome

Union Station

Old Custom House

Duncan Plaza

Aquarium of the Americas

Blaine Kern's Mardi Gras World

Ferry

ALGIERS

Tulane University

Loyola University

UNIVERSITY DISTRICT

Jefferson Ave.

State St. Dr.

LaSalle St.

Louisiana Ave.

CENTRAL BUSINESS DISTRICT

Howard

Confederate Museum

Contemporary Arts Center

WAREHOUSE DISTRICT

Ernest N. Morial Convention Center

Crescent City Connection

Franklin St.

AUDUBON PARK

Wedding Cake House

Milton H. Latter Memorial Library

Christ Church Cathedral

GARDEN DISTRICT

Carroll-Crawford House

Commander's Palace

St. Charles Ave.

Jackson Ave.

McDONOGHVILLE

Audubon Zoological Gardens

Magazine St.

Jefferson Ave.

Perrier St.

Laurel St.

Napoleon Ave.

Louisiana Ave.

Laurel St.

Tchoupitulas St.

Louisiana State Fire Museum

Stumph Blvd.

West Bank Expwy.

Tchoupitulas St.

Tchoupitulas St.

Jackson Ferry

Gretna

Lafayette St.

Gretna Blvd.

Mississippi River

Harvey

4th St.

West Bank Expwy.

Stumph Blvd.

Welcome!

The Big Easy has always had its share of admirers. Celebrated in song, in books, and on the silver screen, few other cities in the world can match New Orleans in terms of charm or architecture. Or good cooking, for that matter. "The most cosmopolitan of provincial towns," wrote Charles Dudley Warren in 1881, and this is still true. Despite its world-wide reputation, this city of music and mystique still retains a small-town feel, easily negotiable by foot, by bus or that most desirable form of transportation – by streetcar.

In these pages Insight's specialist on New Orleans, Honey Naylor, has designed four full-day and eight half-day itineraries to help visitors get the most out of the Crescent City during a short stay. The full days incorporate what Honey considers to be the most outstanding sights, while at the same time offering a comprehensive overview of the city that extends all the way out to Lake Pontchartrain. The half-day tours are designed to appeal to a range of different tastes, and to accommodate visitors with a little more time. Supporting these are sections on history and culture, eating out, nightlife and practical information, including hotels.

Honey Naylor lived and worked in a beautiful apartment in New Orleans's French Quarter for many years before writing this book for us, where she contributed to a variety of publications. She now lives in northern Louisiana, in the home in which she was born. In this book her aim has been to guide visitors not only to the city's well-known attractions, but also to some of the delightful and hidden corners that she has discovered through years of research.

C O N T E N T S

History & Culture

From the French explorers who settled along the Mississippi River to the Spanish takeover of the territory through to the Louisiana Purchase, the history of New Orleans is also the history of Colonial America. The effects of the Civil War, Reconstruction and then prosperity in the 20th century; this is an introduction to the events and personalities that have shaped the city's history **10**

New Orleans Highlights

12 itineraries showing you the best of New Orleans. Begin in the French Quarter, then take a tour of the Garden District. See the Central Business District (CBD), the nerve center of New Orleans. Finally, conclude your first four days with a leisurely, languid drive along the lake. Eight half-day tours follow, to pick and mix depending on your tastes and your timetable

Pages 2/3:
Mardi Gras
merrymakers

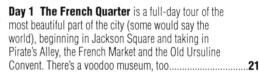 Pick & Mix Itineraries

Pages 8/9: Jackson Square transportation

In 1682, Louis XIV was uninterested when informed of the territory that had been claimed, and subsequently named, for him in the New World. The Sun King was preoccupied. After all, he had around 19 million people to look after, not a few of whom were his mistresses, and he was also having dealings with the Habsburgs and the Huguenots. At the same time, the Grand Monarch was busy moving into his new accommodations, a palace at Versailles.

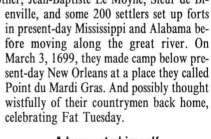

That same year, across the seas, the Frenchman René-Robert Cavalier, Sieur de La Salle, was himself a busy man. He and some other explorers canoed down the Mississippi River to the Gulf of Mexico, and there, on April 9, 1682, planted a cross and unfurled the *fleur-de-lis*. Claiming for France all of the territory drained by the river, he christened it "Louisiane," for his king.

Pierre Le Moyne

Seventeen years elapsed before Louis followed up on La Salle's discovery. He dispatched a group headed by Pierre Le Moyne, Sieur d'Iberville, to explore the Gulf region more fully.

Iberville, with his brother, Jean-Baptiste Le Moyne, Sieur de Bienville, and some 200 settlers set up forts in present-day Mississippi and Alabama before moving along the great river. On March 3, 1699, they made camp below present-day New Orleans at a place they called Point du Mardi Gras. And possibly thought wistfully of their countrymen back home, celebrating Fat Tuesday.

A Law unto himself

As every Louisiana schoolchild learns, Iberville was the founder of Louisiana, and Bienville the founder of New Orleans. True Creoles, the brothers were full-blooded Frenchmen, born in the colonies – in their case, Montreal. The history

John Law

books, though, gloss over the man who was most instrumental in colonizing the Louisiana Territory. That's because John Law was a crook, a sycophantic Scot who fled Britain for France and, in the early 1700s, oiled his way into the inner circle of the Bourbon court. He ingratiated himself with another shady character, Philippe II, duc d'Orléans, who was regent to young Louis XV.

In a complex get-rich-quick scheme that came to be called the Mississippi Bubble, Law gained total control over all of France's colonial finances. Lured by the promise of great riches, settlers poured into the new territory, increasing the colony's population from about 400 in 1717 to about 8,000 in 1721.

Law's finaglings eventually bankrupted France, and he himself disappeared. But before the Bubble burst, the long arm of Law extended, metaphorically at least, across the seas. After obtaining from the Crown a charter to exploit the Louisiana Territory, Law appointed Bienville to establish a settlement and to name it after the duke – la Nouvelle Orléans. In 1717, Bienville selected for the colony a crescent-shaped piece of turf at a great bend in the Mississippi, 110 miles (180km) upriver from the Gulf of Mexico. With Law gone, France was left with a huge chunk of New World real estate – land thought to be worthless.

Criminals and slaves

This new colony, far away, seemed the ideal place in which to dump sundry miscreants, thus cleaning up Parisian streets and emptying Parisian prisons. In the 1720s, Bienville complained to the duke about the unsavory, even dangerous, folks he was being sent to populate the colony, and so the government recruited 10,000 German settlers (only about 2,000 actually made it to the territory).

By 1720, the first group of slaves had arrived. Bienville promulgated the *Code Noir*, laying down penalties ranging from branding and mutilation to death for crimes such as escaping or striking a white, but also compelling masters to feed and clothe their slaves and instruct them in Catholicism. Freed slaves, however, were given the same rights and privileges as those enjoyed by the free-born.

Slave auction

The frontier community was dogged by political and religious discord, and by deteriorating relations with the local Indians. This culminated in a massacre in 1729 of about 250 colonists and slaves by Natchez Indians. Bienville mounted two unsuccessful campaigns against the aggressive Chickasaws, but a truce was not reached until the early 1740s, by which time a despondent Bienville, too weary to continue, returned permanently to France.

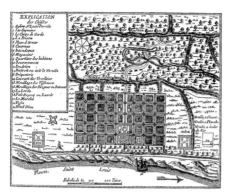

Female influences

But there were stabilizing influences, too. In 1727, for example, 12 Sisters of Ursula came to the colony to establish a school for girls and to care for the sick. Their convent not yet complete, the sisters stayed elsewhere until they could move into their new home. The Old Ursuline Convent on Chartres Street, completed in 1752 and one of the oldest extant buildings in the Lower Mississippi Valley, is the second convent to sit on that site.

In 1728, the French government sent a group of respectable young ladies as brides to the settlers, providing each with a little chest packed with a trousseau. Because the chests were known in French as *cassettes*, their bearers became known as Casket Girls.

Once on its feet, New Orleans, as a French Crown colony, took on many of the trappings of the Bourbon court. The well-known Orleanian love for partying dates from the earliest colonial days. Culture followed; opera, for example, was first performed in North America in New Orleans, with a 1791 production of *Sylvain*.

Spain takes over

Politically, though, there was turbulence. The Louisiana Territory was a serious loss-maker as far as investors and the French monarchy were concerned and in 1763 it was ceded by secret treaty to Spain (whose king, Carlos III, was Louis XV's cousin). The French Colonials, horrified when news reached them of the transfer, staged a mighty protest. The revolt was put down by the Spanish commander, General Alejandro O'Reilly, and his 2,600 troops. The leaders of the resistance were shot, and la Nouvelle Orléans became la Nueva Orleans. But, although the new governors were Spanish, few other Spaniards opted to move to the New World and, for the most part, the colony's 3,200 citizens retained their Gallic values.

Although O'Reilly has often been presented in the history books as a cruel despot – "Bloody O'Reilly" – his rule was more firm than fearsome and the colony prospered. Trade with France and the French West Indies was encouraged, and a blind eye was turned to smuggling and the illegal but profitable trade with the British in West Florida. The population rose to about 5,000.

Two catastrophic fires swept through the town in the late 1700s, during the Spanish Colonial period. The first, in 1788, destroyed four-fifths of the buildings. The citizens had scarcely recovered when another fire broke out in 1794. Because it was rebuilt by Spaniards, the French Quarter has a decidedly Spanish look, incorporating inner courtyards or patios. Masonry replaced wood as the main building material, and ceramic tiles were preferred to shingles on roofs. Most of the buildings seen today date from the mid-19th century.

The French return

The French Revolution of 1789 and the war between France and Spain in 1793 stirred passions among the French Creoles, the descendents of the original settlers. But the wealthy landowners supported the status quo and republican sentiments were further diluted by the arrival of French nobility fleeing the post-revolutionary purges in Paris.

It wasn't just French nobles who became interested in this flourishing port city. Napoleon Bonaparte, having consolidated his power in France, began dreaming of an overseas empire. In 1800 he persuaded Spain to retrocede the Louisiana Territory to France. This alarmed President Thomas Jefferson, who saw a threat to trade, and some Congressmen favored seizing the port. Napoleon realized that the colony would be difficult to defend indefinitely and he decided to sell not only New Orleans but also the whole of Louisiana to the United States. Negotiations were concluded speedily in 1803; the price was $15 million.

The 8,000 citizens, somewhat bewildered at the town's changing fortunes, were less than enthusiastic about the new order, but at least they were relieved to be spared the threat that the anti-Catholic measures then sweeping France might be imported into their corner of the New World. In 1804, Louisiana was divided, with the boundaries of the Territory of Orleans corresponding to those of the present state. In 1805, New Orleans, in essence a small provincial town with about 1,300 buildings, was incorporated as a city, and in 1812 Louisiana was admitted into the Union.

The territory was little affected by the war declared in 1812 between the US and Britain. But it did become the scene of the conflict's only major American victory when, in what became known as the Battle of New Orleans, General Andrew Jackson decisively repulsed an attempted invasion by the British on January 8, 1815.

Gracious living

A period of prosperity

By the 1830s, the town had entered its Golden Age. After the Louisiana Purchase, Americans had come pouring downriver, and New Orleans became a boom town. Snubbed by the Creoles of the French Quarter, the Americans built grand mansions upriver of the Quarter, on the grounds of former sugar plantations, extending ever farther upriver. The economy was fueled by trade as goods from the Mississippi valley were shipped to New Orleans by the newly introduced steamboats, to be transferred to vessels bound for Asia and Europe.

By 1840, New Orleans was the fourth largest city in the country – with a population of 80,000 – and one of the wealthiest. Palatial hotels were built, the streets and sidewalks were paved, and gas lighting was introduced by James Caldwell, a British actor, entrepreneur and politician who had established an English-speaking theater in the city.

The Creole culture was clearly under threat. The increasingly middle-class Anglo-American professionals who arrived showed no interest in learning French, and even the new immigrants from France regarded the Creoles with a certain *hauteur*. In 1836 the Americans decisively weakened the power of the Creoles by persuading the state legislature to tear up the city's charter and divide it into three municipalities. In 1852, the municipalities were reunited, consolidating American domination, and the occasion was marked by a carnival parade – the model for a famous tradition.

Power was still denied to freed slaves, even though they had more legal rights than free blacks in most Southern states. The laws restricting their rights were often not enforced, however, and the laws governing slaves were also largely ignored – a few even owned and carried guns with the full knowledge of their masters.

The War Between the States

Gradually, the city's commercial base began to be eroded. The Erie Canal, opened in the 1830s, began to divert commerce away from the Mississippi and towards the east and New York. The trend increased when the railroads reached Chicago in the 1850s. Even so, the Golden Age lasted until 1861, when the War Between the States (as Southerners call the Civil War) began and Louisiana, with 10 other Southern states, seceded from the Union. New Orleans was among the first Southern cities to fall to Union forces, having surrendered in 1862. Federal troops were not warmly welcomed, especially by the city's womenfolk, and the famous Order No. 28 was issued, warning that any woman insulting a Federal soldier could expect "to be treated as a woman of the town plying her vocation."

The war ended in 1865, but Louisiana suffered under Reconstruction until 1877 when the last Federal troops left. With the other former Confederate states, Louisiana was slow in recovering from the devastation of the war. Then the construction of new jetties at the river's mouth and the coming of the railways combined to boost trade, and New Orleans became the nation's main center for the distribution of cotton and sugar. Social enlightenment did not match economic progress, however: in the 1890s, racial segregation in Louisiana was legally sanctioned.

The 20th century

In an attempt to control rampant prostitution, the city administration in 1897 restricted such activity to an area of about 20 blocks just beyond the city's

An officer and a gentleman

Civil War banknote

old French Quarter. This became known as Storyville – to the chagrin of councilman Sidney Story, who was responsible for the legislation – and in the early years of the new century the region nurtured a number of local jazz musicians such as King Oliver, Jelly Roll Morton and Louis Armstrong. Their inspired playing created one of the city's most enduring images.

But another city image was under threat. By the 1920s much of the old French Quarter had become a slum and centuries-old buildings were being demolished to create parking lots. Concerned citizens pioneered a preservation movement, but it wasn't until 1936 that the state set up the Vieux Carré Commission – the first body of its kind in the United States – with powers to protect buildings of architectural and historic value. Job creation schemes initiated by President Franklin D. Roosevelt during the Depression of the 1930s aided the reclamation process.

Being an important port, New Orleans was given special protection during World War II, when enemy German submarines were operating in the Gulf of Mexico. After the war, under Mayor Chep Morrison, massive road and office building programs transformed the city, aided by oil revenues. Oil had first been discovered near Jennings in 1901 and, in 1947, the first offshore oil well off Louisiana's gulf coast heralded the state's lucrative offshore oil and gas industry which brought prosperity for nearly 40 years.

Celebrating St Patrick's Day

In the 1970s and '80s, as conventional industries were facing tough times, the importance of tourism – today an industry worth more than $2 billion a year – was acknowledged. One of the early exponents of this new source of revenue was the city's first black mayor, Ernest N. "Dutch" Morial. After his sudden death in 1989, a second black mayor, Sidney Barthelemy, promoted the city's riverfront development, introduced a European-style gambling casino, and went after the lucrative convention business. Dutch Morial's son, Marc, continued these policies when he became mayor in 1994 and initiated major social and environmental campaigns.

New Orleans's reputation as a party town is as well earned as it is well known. Mardi Gras is the biggest blow-out in all of North America, and there are scores of other local festivals such as the spring Jazz Fest. New Orleanians adore their city, and when there is no particular festival to celebrate, the city simply celebrates itself.

Historical Highlights

1541 Spaniard Hernando De Soto is first known European to see the Mississippi River.

1682 La Salle's expedition arrives at mouth of Mississippi River; he claims the country for Louis XIV.

1699 Iberville establishes posts at Mobile and Biloxi; explores Mississippi River northward; returns to France leaving Bienville in charge.

1701 Bienville becomes governor of the Louisiana Territory, and makes Mobile his headquarters.

1717 French Government grants John Law's company a charter for control of Louisiana.

1718 Bienville selects site for his headquarters on the Mississippi River, and names it after the Duke of Orleans.

1719 First large importation of slaves arrives in New Orleans.

1720 John Law's companies fail, and France is bankrupt; Law forced to flee France in disgrace.

1721 French engineers lay out streets of New Orleans.

1722 Capital of territory moves to New Orleans.

1727 First Ursuline nuns arrive and open a convent, where they teach Indians, black women and white girls.

1728 The Casket Girls arrive and are looked after by the Sisters of Ursula until their marriages.

1731 Louisiana becomes a colony of the crown.

1743 Bienville leaves for France, never to return to Louisiana, and is succeeded in his post by the Marquis de Vaudreuil.

1762 Louis XV cedes Louisiana to Spain by secret treaty of Fontainbleau; but the transfer not announced until 1764.

1763 The Treaty of Paris confirms the cession of Louisiana to Spain.

1766 Don Antonio de Ulloa arrives to rule Louisiana in the name of the Spanish king. Hundreds of Orleanians revolt in protest.

1768 Creole leaders demand that Ulloa be banished. Ulloa leaves for Cuba, Louisiana becomes an independent state.

1769 Count Alejandro O'Reilly arrives with 2,000 troops to rule for Spain; leaders of Louisiana province swear allegiance to the Spanish crown. Five leaders of revolt against Ulloa executed in New Orleans.

1779 Spain enters war against England; Spanish king authorizes Louisiana subjects to begin operations against English.

1780 Spain gains control of all original Louisiana Territory.

1788 Fire destroys almost all New Orleans buildings.

1793 Pope Pius VI establishes Diocese of Louisiana.

1794 Fire in New Orleans destroys 200 buildings. The rebuilt New Orleans Church of St Louis dedicated as cathedral.

1795 Treaty between Spain and the United States grants Americans free navigation of the Mississippi. In New Orleans, Etienne de Bore successfully granulates sugar on his plantation in what is now Audubon Park. Cabildo built as seat of Spanish colonial administration.

1796 Spanish governor Carondelet establishes first police force and street lighting system in New Orleans.

1799 Spanish discontinue right of deposit at port of New Orleans.

1800 Secret Treaty of Ildefonso provides for retrocession of Louisiana from Spain to France.

1802 Spain closes port of New Orleans to American commerce.

1803 French announce transfer of Louisiana from Spain to France. President Jefferson buys Louisiana Territory for $15 million.

1805 New Orleans is incorporated as a city.

1812 Louisiana is at last admitted to the Union.

1815 General Andrew Jackson defeats British troops in Battle of New Orleans.

1830 State government moves from New Orleans to Donaldsonville.

1831 State government moves back

to New Orleans. First railroad west of Alleghenies, the Pontchartrain Railroad, opens service between New Orleans and Milenburg.

1835 The New Orleans & Carrollton Railroad (later the St Charles Streetcar line) begins operation.

1836 Ill-feeling between Creoles and Americans causes division of city into three municipalities.

1838 The first Mardi Gras parade takes place on Fat Tuesday on the streets of the city.

1849 Baton Rouge replaces New Orleans as state capital. The Southern Yacht Club opens. Baroness Pontalba begins work on Pontalba Buildings.

1851 Under the auspices of promotor P.T. Barnum, Jenny Lind sings in New Orleans.

1852 The three municipalities are again consolidated into one city that now includes the town of Lafayette.

1853 More than 11,000 people in New Orleans die of yellow fever.

1859 The French Opera House in New Orleans opens.

1861 Louisiana secedes, joins Confederate States of America.

1862 New Orleans one of the first Southern cities to fall to the Union.

1865 The Civil War ends.

1867 Fifth Military District (formerly Louisiana and Texas) headquarters in New Orleans.

1868 Louisiana readmitted to Union with new state constitution.

1870 Historic steamboat race between the *Natchez* and the *Robert E. Lee* begins in New Orleans.

1872 Rex organization parades for first time on Fat Tuesday.

1874 Town of Carrollton incorporated into New Orleans. White League defeats New Orleans Metropolitan Police in "Battle of Liberty Place."

1877 Reconstruction ends, federal troops leave New Orleans. Birth of Buddy Bolden, the man credited with first playing jazz.

1883 The first through train from New Orleans to California begins operation.

1884-85 World's Industrial & Cotton Centennial Exposition is held in New Orleans.

1892 "Gentleman Jim" Corbett knocks out John L. Sullivan in New Orleans to win world championship.

1911 Loyola Academy and the College of the Immaculate Conception join to become Loyola University.

1915 The name "jazz" is given to New Orleans music when introduced in Chicago.

1919 French Opera House destroyed by fire.

1957 The 24-mile (38km) Lake Pontchartrain Causeway opens.

1958 The Greater New Orleans Bridge opens.

1965 New Orleans Saints team joins National Football League.

1974 A new state constitution is adopted.

1975 Louisiana Superdome opens.

1977 Ernest N. ("Dutch") Morial is elected the first black mayor of New Orleans.

1984 Louisiana World Exposition is held.

1991 Riverboat gambling on Mississippi River and state waterways is legalized. Carnival krewes Comus, Momus and Proteus cease parading as result of city anti-discrimination ordinance.

1993 State casino board awards Harrah's Jazz Co. a license to operate Louisiana's only land-based casino in New Orleans.

1994 Hotel building boom begins with announcement of major expansion of Ernest N. Morial Convention Center in New Orleans. Riverboat gambling on a fairly major scale is introduced in New Orleans.

1995 Rivergate Exhibition Hall demolished to make way for Harrah's Casino New Orleans. Temporary Harrah's casino opens in Armstrong Park.

1996 Harrah's declares bankruptcy, closes temporary casino six months after opening, ceases construction of land-based casino. In state-wide referendum on gambling, voters give approval to existing riverboat casinos, reject video poker and further casino development.

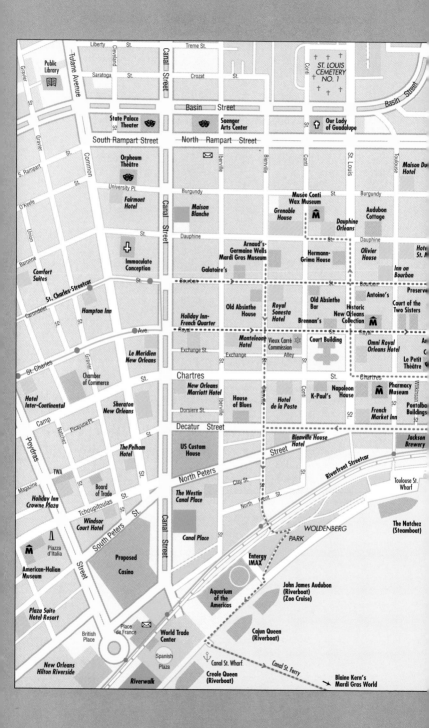

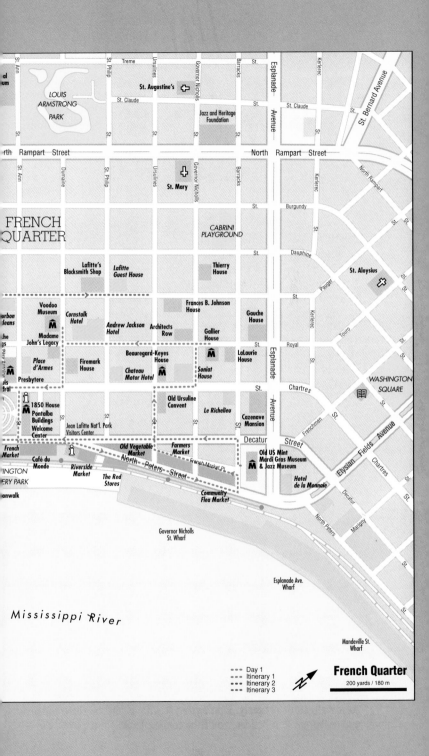

French Quarter

200 yards / 180 m

--- Day 1
--- Itinerary 1
--- Itinerary 2
--- Itinerary 3

Day Itineraries

The curves in the Mississippi River render ordinary compass points useless. Resourceful Orleanians refer to uptown (upriver), downtown (downriver), lakeside (toward Lake Pontchartrain), and riverside. Canal Street is the dividing line between uptown and downtown. Below Canal Street is downtown; above is uptown. Mid-City lies in the big bowl-shaped area between the outer edge of the French Quarter and City Park.

New Orleans developed along the Mississippi: when the French Quarter became overcrowded, Faubourg Marigny began to develop downriver, below Esplanade Avenue. The present Central Business District (CBD) evolved from what was called the American Sector: as the Americans began pouring in after the 1803 Louisiana Purchase, they were snubbed by the French, and began to build upriver of present-day Canal Street, where former sugar plantations were subdivided into lots. Following the river farther and farther up, the Garden District grew out of the enormous Livaudais Plantation; later the towns of Lafayette and Carrollton were incorporated. Algiers (across river, so to speak, from the Quarter and CBD) is a very old residential section.

Jaws, French Market

Our tours are divided into two parts. The Day Itineraries focus on the main sights in the French Quarter, the CBD, the Garden District and the Lakefront. The Pick & Mix tours cover other aspects which, in many cases, can be combined with a Day Itinerary or other Pick & Mix tours. The French Quarter, also called the Vieux Carré, meaning "old square," is the city's oldest neighborhood. In 1721, French engineers laid out the streets in a rectangular grid, six blocks deep, 13 blocks wide. You can walk its square mile in less than three hours, but it can take weeks to investigate it properly. Don't rush; it will all still be there when you wake up, and besides, you'll be coming back. Most people do.

Café du Monde

The French Quarter

Romantic, charming and wildly popular, for some people the French Quarter is New Orleans. Laid out in a perfect grid, the Quarter is a mere six blocks deep and 13 blocks wide, but its famous attractions are celebrated in song and on the screen.
See map on pages 18-19

The French Quarter's official borders, as defined by the Vieux Carré Commission, are the downtown side of Iberville Street, the riverside of Rampart Street, the uptown side of Esplanade Avenue, and Decatur Street. Contrary to what most people think, including many Orleanians, the 100 block of the French Quarter is not actually in the French Quarter. That block between Canal and Iberville streets is not under the jurisdiction of the VCC, which is why there is, for example, a McDonald's in the 100 block of Royal Street, and across the street from it a store called American Junk ("We Sell Yesterday," they say). It would practically be a capital offense for a fast-food chain to appear on, for instance, the 200 block of Royal Street.

The Vieux Carré Commission was created in 1936 by the state legislature, and charged with preserving the Quarter. The Commission came about as a result of heavy lobbying by local

21

preservationists who saw that the whole area was in danger of decaying. In fact, the Quarter as we see it today did not come into being until after World War II. In his marvelous book *Fabulous New Orleans*, published in 1928 and reissued in 1988, Lyle Saxon describes the French Quarter of the Teens and Twenties, using words such as "tenements" and "squalor," along with "charm." The Commission is known for driving a hard bargain regarding change, and imposes heavy fines for any unauthorized alterations. There is a long-standing moratorium on construction, which is why all new hotels are in other areas.

Buildings and houses in the Quarter are small, most of them from one to three storys, and sit shoulder to shoulder flush with the *banquette* – a creole word meaning sidewalk. Painted in pretty ice-cream colors, they are further dressed with dormer windows, gables, gingerbread trim, or lacy iron-work balconies or galleries. (A balcony is supported by brackets; a gallery is supported by slender colonettes.) Baskets of ferns and flowers dangle from most eaves, and almost all have hidden courtyards awash with banana trees, palms and subtropical plants. Magnolia trees abound – there is a beauty on the grounds of the Supreme Court Building at 400 Royal Street. Street signs on lamp-posts are in French and English, and plaques on the buildings proclaim the Spanish versions. Dauphine Street is also Rue Dauphine and Camino de Bayona.

You can get a good perspective of **Jackson Square** and the Mississippi River from **Washington Artillery Park** on Decatur Street. Ramps and steps lead from the street to the "park" (concrete), which was named for the celebrated 141st Artillery. The river, busy with the water traffic of a major port, flows along one side of the park. You can get close to it on **Moonwalk**, a promenade with benches and river breezes. With your back to the river, you'll look out over Jackson Square.

The French Creoles designed their new Orleans along the lines of a medieval French village: the centerpiece was the town square, and on it sat the church and government buildings. Jackson Square, called by the Creoles the Place d'Armes, was a public gathering place as well as a militia parade ground. It was renamed in 1851 to honor Andrew Jackson, the hero of the 1815 Battle of New Orleans which was fought five miles downriver of New Orleans. The grand equestrian statue of Jackson was carved by Clark Mills; Jackson himself dedicated the monument in 1856.

The triple-steepled **St Louis Cathedral** rises up between the Cabildo, on your left, and

St Louis Cathedral

the Presbytère. Named for France's saint-king, Louis IX, the cathedral is the third church on this site. The first two were destroyed by hurricane and by fire, respectively. The building fund for the present church was courtesy of Don Andres Almonester y Roxas, a wealthy Spanish philanthropist whose generosity greatly enhanced the colony. The church was dedicated as a cathedral in 1794. The mural behind the main altar, of Saint Louis announcing the Seventh Crusade, was painted in 1872 by Erasme Humbrecht; it has since been refurbished. In 1964, Pope Paul VI designated the cathedral a Minor Basilica. The flagstone mall in front of the church was named Jean Paul Deux, in honor of Pope John Paul II's 1987 visit.

The Cabildo and Presbytère are almost identical twins; both were built in the 1790s, both replaced earlier structures, and both were funded by the philanthropic Almonester. The **Cabildo**, which was built to house the Spanish town council, is one of the state's most important buildings. Transfer papers for the Louisiana Purchase were signed here in 1803. In 1825, the Marquis de Lafayette stayed here on his triumphant tour of the country. When the city was divided into three separate municipalities in the 19th century, the Cabildo served as city hall for the First Municipality. It later housed the Louisiana Supreme Court. Now a museum, the Cabildo contains important documents and artifacts pertaining to Louisiana's multicultural history. There is even a death mask of Napoleon, one of only three in the world.

Saluting history

On the downriver side of the Cathedral, the **Presbytère** is almost a mirror image of the Cabildo. This building never served its original purpose, which was to be the rectory for the priests of the cathedral. The city bought it in the early 19th century, and during the 1830s it was used as a courthouse. Now it is a museum with changing exhibits.

Another building in the Louisiana State Museum complex is the **Louisiana State Arsenal**, behind the Cabildo at 615 St Peter. This was the site of the *calabozo*, or prison, in the Spanish Colonial period. After the Louisiana Purchase of 1803, when the Americans gained jurisdiction, a state arsenal was built here. The building was headquarters for the Louisiana Legion, a militia unit, whose insignia and initials are worked into the wrought-iron railing on the Pirate Alley side of the building.

St Peter and St Ann streets, which border the square, are lined with the identical **Pontalba Buildings**. Among the nation's oldest apartment houses, these three-story redbrick buildings were constructed between 1849 and 1851, sometimes literally, by the Baroness Micaela Pontalba. Micaela was the daughter of the city's benefactor, Don Andres Almonester y Roxas. In a period when Americans were flocking into town, and building (and trading) upriver of the Quarter, the Baroness built the Pontalbas in an attempt to bring trade back to the Quarter. Then, as now, the Pontalbas have shops on the ground floor and apartments above. The Pontalbas are graced with some of the most beautiful cast-iron in town; note that the initials AP, for Almonester and Pontalba, are worked into the design. One of the restored townhouses, the **1850 House** at 523 St Ann, is maintained by the Louisiana State Museum, and gives visitors a

Le Petit Théâtre

chance to see how upper-class Creoles lived in the 19th century. As well as canopied beds and other antique furniture, the apartment contains a kitchen filled with old-timey things and a display of antique dolls.

Across St Peter Street from the Cabildo is a balconied pink stucco building that houses **Le Petit Théâtre du Vieux Carré**, the oldest continually operating community theater in America. It began in 1916 with a group called The Drawing Room Players, who first mounted their productions in a private home and later moved to space in the lower Pontalbas. In 1919, the company moved to its present location.

The building that houses the theater is a faithful reconstruction of one that was completed on this site in 1797. The interior of the theater has a charming old-world ambience, and the inner courtyard is lovely. Each season between September and June the theater presents seven plays, including musicals, on its main stage, as well as performances for kids that are held in the Children's Corner.

Up the street from Le Petit, at 632 St Peter, a plaque notes that Tennessee Williams wrote the play *A Streetcar Named Desire* in an apartment in this building. Williams scholars say the playwright was inspired by the streetcar that used to rattle down Royal Street. Williams first arrived in New Orleans in 1939; many years later he bought a house on nearby Dumaine Street, and continued until his death to visit the city he called "my spiritual home."

Just around the corner from the theater, on Chartres Street, is yet another New Orleans institution. **La Marquise** pastry shop is a French pâtisserie with wonderful croissants, Napoleons, éclairs, coffees and other delectations. There are a few tables in the two tiny rooms and a pleasant courtyard with umbrellas to shield against the sun's rays. La Marquise is a delightful interlude in anyone's day.

The flagstone alleyways on each side of the Cathedral – **Père Antoine Alley** on its downriver side and **Pirate's Alley** on the

Anybody got a Quarter?

other – were cut in the 1830s. Father Antonio de Sedella was a Spanish priest much loved by the Creoles, who called him Père Antoine. At 624 Pirate's Alley, the building that now houses **Faulkner House Books** is where William Faulkner wrote his first novel. Behind the church, **Cathedral Gardens** (sometimes called St Anthony's Gardens) is a small landscaped park where many a duel was fought in the early colonial days. The statue is the Sacred Heart of Jesus; behind it is a monument, erected on the orders of the naval minister to Napoleon III, honoring 30 French sailors who died in 1857 in a yellow fever epidemic.

La Madeleine, opposite the Presbytère on St Ann Street, serves light lunches; at the **Central Grocery Store** on Decatur Street you can buy a *muffuletta* to go, and eat it on the Moonwalk promenade. (*Muffulettas* are Italian sandwiches the size of frisbees; be advised to order a quarter portion unless you think you'll never have a chance to eat again.) **Café du Monde** at St Ann and Decatur is open 24 hours for *café au lait* and *beignets*.

The building that houses the Café du Monde is one of the oldest in the **French Market**. The early settlers came to the market to buy food and goods; even before, in the late 1600s, there was a trading post here. Now it's a festive marketplace, with shops, ice-cream parlors and open-air cafés stretching down to Barracks Street. At the market's farthest downriver point, the **Farmer's Market** is awash with fresh produce and fruits.

Gallier House interior

From the French Market, walk up Ursulines Street to Chartres Street. The **Old Ursuline Convent** is one of the oldest edifices in the lower Mississippi Valley. It was begun in 1745 on the orders of Louis XV, to replace an earlier convent on this site, and completed in 1752. An example of pure French Colonial architecture, it is the only undisputed survivor of the late 18th-century fires. The first Sisters of Ursula arrived in New Orleans in 1727, bringing with them from Rouen the iron cross that's displayed in the courtyard. Guided tours take in sundry documents and artifacts, and the lovely **St Mary's Church**. After his 1815 victory in the Battle of New Orleans, Andrew Jackson came here to thank the sisters for their prayers.

One block away on Royal Street, the **Gallier House** is a handsomely restored building dating from 1857. The house was designed by the renowned architect James Gallier Jr, who lived there with his family.

Two blocks toward the CBD, the **Voodoo Museum** on Dumaine Street is an only-in-New-Orleans phenomenon. Small and dimly lit, the museum displays voodoo potions and dolls, memorabilia related to the 19th-century voodoo queen Marie Laveau, and an al-

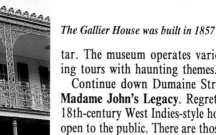

The Gallier House was built in 1857

tar. The museum operates various walking tours with haunting themes.

Continue down Dumaine Street to see **Madame John's Legacy**. Regrettably this 18th-century West Indies-style house is not open to the public. There are those who believe that the original house on this site, built in 1724, was not completely leveled in the 1788 fire, and thus predates the convent and deserves the "oldest" trophy. "Madame John" was a fictional character in a short story by the 19th-century writer George Washington Cable.

Cut through Jackson Square to reach the **Napoleon House**, one of New Orleans's most treasured watering holes. Parts of the building date from the late 18th century. In the early 19th century it was the home of New Orleans mayor Nicholas Girod, who was among the local admirers of Napoleon Bonaparte and organized a syndicate with the intention of rescuing the former emperor from his exile on St Helena. Girod even added a third story to his house to provide accommodation for the Little Corporal. A schooner was dispatched, but Napoleon died before he could be saved. The bar and adjoining **Girod House** restaurant are decorated with Napoleonic memorabilia. Grueling research has established that a person can while away hours in the bar, knocking back Pimms Cups (the house drink) and listening to taped classical music.

To reach the **Hermann-Grima House**, walk away from the river to the corner of St Louis and Bourbon streets. (En route you'll pass by **Antoine's**, the city's oldest and most famous French Creole restaurant.) The Hermann-Grima House was built in 1831 for a wealthy merchant named Samuel Hermann. Judge Felix Grima bought it in 1844, and it remained in the Grima family for five generations. Guided tours include the parterre gardens and outbuildings, where Creole cooking demonstrations take place on Thursdays in winter.

Voodoo tableau at Musée Conti

To reach the **Musée Conti Wax Museum**, walk one block up St Louis Street to Dauphine Street, turn left for one block and then right on Conti Street. A well-executed wax museum, the Musée Conti displays "Louisiana Legends" – everyone from La Salle to Andrew Jackson to Marie Laveau – in historically accurate tableaux.

Garden District Tour

Fragrant, fanciful and filled with flowers, the Garden District is possibly the city's most beautiful neighborhood. It is as sprawling as the French Quarter is compact.

Board the St Charles Streetcar at Canal and Carondelet streets in the Central Business District and rumble up the avenue to First Street, which is stop 14. (The streetcar itself, which follows the route of the railroad and is the world's oldest continuously operating street railway system, is a National Historic Landmark.)

Morris-Israel House

The elegant and stately Greek Revival mansion at 2265 First Street is the **Dabney-O'Meallie House**, designed by architect James Gallier Jr in 1857. This was the same year that he built his own home in the French Quarter.

Walk along First Street one block away from the streetcar tracks toward the river. At 2340 Prytania Street, **Toby's Corner** (also called the Toby-Westfeldt House) is a raised cottage dating from about 1838, and said to be the oldest house in the Garden District. "Raised cottage" refers to a style of house in which the living quarters are on the upper level, as a protection against flooding.

Across the way, at 2343 Prytania Street, is the **Louise McGehee School**, an exclusive girls' school which is housed in a Second Empire mansion that was built in 1872,

Garden District

300 yards / 270 m

Danneel St · Washington · 3rd · Dryates · 4th · Philip St · Baronne Av · 2nd · Josephine St · St Andrew · St Mary · St Charles Avenue

Pontchartrain Hotel
Avenue Plaza Hotel and Spa
Ramada Hotel-St. Charles
Carondelet · Prytania

Baronne · Grima House · Bradish Johnson House · Jackson Avenue
Carondelet · Briggs-Staub House · Our Mother of Perpetual Help · Toby's Corner · The Seven Sisters
Christ Church Cathedral · The Rink · Opera Association · Morris-Israel House
St Charles Av · Washington · Colonel Short's Villa · Robinson House · Carroll-Crawford House
Coliseum · Musson-Bell House · Brevard House
LAFAYETTE CEMETERY NO. 1 · Commander's Palace · Montgomery-Hero House · Payne-Strachan House

GARDEN DISTRICT

George Washington Cable House · Camp · Magazine Av · Washington · Constance · 1st · 2nd · 3rd · 4th

Harmony · Coliseum · Chestnut · 6th · 7th St · Magazine · 8th St · Constance · Laurel St · Laurel Av · Annunciation · BURKE PARK

MONTIERO · Camp · Pleasant

during Reconstruction, as a home for planter Bradish Johnson. Further down First Street, the **Morris-Israel House** (No. 1331) and its near neighbor the **Carroll-Crawford House** (No. 1315) are Italianate mansions rich in ironwork, both designed by Samuel Jamison in 1869.

At the corner of Chestnut, 1239 First Street is **Brevard House**, the home of novelist Anne Rice and one of several Garden District properties owned by the Vampire Chronicler. There are often some Rice fans staked out in front, hoping for a glimpse of their idol. The house, prominently featured in her bestseller *The Witching Hour*, dates from 1857, and was restored by Anne and her husband, poet-artist Stan.

The imposing **Payne-Strahan House,** at 1134 First Street, was the home of Judge Jacob Strahan for whom it was built in 1849. In 1889, Strahan's friend, Jefferson Davis, the president of the Confederacy, became ill while traveling through New Orleans and was brought to this house, where he died.

Walk two blocks along Camp Street to Third Street and turn right. The interesting bracket-style **Montgomery-Hero House** at 1213 Third Street is the only one of its kind among all the Garden District's Greek Revival and Italianate mansions. An unknown architect designed the house, which dates from 1868, for Archibald Montgomery, president of the Crescent City Railroad.

In the next block, 1331 Third Street is the Italianate **Musson-Bell House**, built in 1853 for Michel Musson, a New Orleans postmaster who was an uncle of the French Impressionist painter Edgar Degas. (The Degas House on Esplanade Avenue, where the painter stayed for several months in 1872, is now a bed-and-breakfast inn.)

Opera headquarters

The enormous white house at 1415 Third Street, the **Robinson House**, was built in 1864-65, just as the Civil War was ending. It was the home of Walter Robinson, a banker from Virginia. The splendid two-story mansion is said to have been the first Garden District house to have indoor plumbing.

One block farther, back on Prytania Street, turn right to see the marvelous Greek Revival-cum-Queen Anne turreted house at No. 2504. Now headquarters for the **Women's Guild of the New Orleans Opera Association**, the house was built for Edward Davis in 1858. Its last resident was Nettie Seebold, who died in 1955 and left the house in her will to the Guild. It's open for tours to groups of 20 or more.

In 1995, Anne Rice purchased **Our Mother of Perpetual Help**, a former Redemptorist Chapel at 2521 Prytania. A lovely place, it was built in the 1850s for Brooklyn native Henry

Lonsdale, who loved New Orleans almost as much as Rice does.

Like the Montgomery-Hero house, the **Briggs-Staub House** at 2605 Prytania is a one-of-a-kind in the Garden District. This one is a fanciful, grand Gothic creation, designed in 1849 by James Gallier Sr for Englishman Charles Briggs. The little guesthouse at its side is an exact copy of the big house.

You can spend the night in the neighboring **Sully Mansion** (2631 Prytania), a lovely 1891 Queen Anne house that's now a bed-and-breakfast inn. And across the street from it, at 1448 Fourth Street, the elegant and quite large **Colonel Short's Villa**, also known as the Short-Favrot House, is an Italianate mansion designed by noted architect Henry Howard. Howard built this house the same year he designed Nottoway Plantation, having completed his work on Madewood Plantation some years previously. Both plantations are west of New Orleans, and are open for tours.

The next street over from Fourth is Washington Avenue (there is no Fifth Street). The high walls at Washington, Sixth, Coliseum, and Prytania streets enclose **Lafayette Cemetery**. This burial ground was first used in the 1830s as the cemetery for the town of Lafayette and through the iron gates you can see the white above-ground tombs that are typical of New Orleans graveyards. Several of Anne Rice's fictional characters have intimate knowledge of this graveyard, and Rice herself launched the book-signing for *Mmenoch the Devil* in Lafayette Cemetery. In full bridal attire, she rode in a casket from the cemetery to the **Garden District Book Shop**, which hosts all of her New Orleans signings.

The book shop is across from the cemetery in **The Rink** (2727 Prytania Street), a small multilevel shopping mall that was built in the 1880s as the Crescent City Skating Rink. If the cemetery has left you thirsty, **P.J.'s** serves no blood but it does have gourmet

Bread pudding soufflé at Commander's Palace

coffees and pastries, and you can at least sit out on the terrace and gaze at the cemetery. As an alternative, you could have a splurge lunch at **Commander's Palace** in a wonderful Victorian mansion. The bread pudding soufflé is to die for.

Farther on, the well-known 19th-century writer George Washington Cable lived in the raised cottage at **1313 Eighth Street**. Mark Twain was among the literary luminaries who were visitors in Cable's Garden District house. Not far away, at 1525 Louisiana Avenue, is the elegant, three-story **Bultman House**. Architect William Freret built it in 1857 as his private residence, and nearly a century later it was the inspiration for the set of Tennessee Williams' *Suddenly, Last Summer*.

A Guide to New Orleans Architecture, published by the local chapter of the American Institute of Architects, is an illustrated paperback in which many Garden District homes are described. Except where noted, these are private residences, and are not open to the public – except during Spring Fiesta when certain home owners allow tours.

Magazine Street borders both the Garden District and the area known as the Irish Channel. Magazine Street is lined with Creole cottages and once-grand Victorian mansions – many of them now antique shops offering pleasant browsing.

Sully Mansion

The **Irish Channel**, like the Garden District, was once a part of the Livaudais Plantation and the City of Lafayette. However, because of its proximity to the wharves along the river, it has always been a tough, working-class neighborhood. The Irish immigrants who flooded into New Orleans in the 1840s settled around Adele Street, which is still the heart of the Channel. About the same time large numbers of Germans also moved into the neighborhood, but for some reason the Channel remained "Irish." The Irish and Germans have since left, and the neighborhood is now predominantly black and Cuban.

The spirit of revitalization that swept through the nearby Warehouse District is gradually seeping into the Channel. But unfortunately for its reputation, the centerpiece of the neighborhood is the St Thomas Street Housing Project, a federal housing project that is dangerous territory both by day and by night. A much better idea is to stick to the streets within the Garden District, or to take the Streetcar Tour instead.

After midnight in the CBD

Central Business District

Reserve a car for tomorrow's drive along the lake. Then, get ready to enjoy the CBD, New Orleans's power center and the home of the Superdome. There is a grand, bird's-eye perspective from Viewpoint, the glass-enclosed observation deck on the 31st floor of the World Trade Center.

The Central Business District (CBD) is separated from the French Quarter by Canal Street, which begins at the foot of the World Trade Center. Canal Street once marked the boundary between the French and the American sectors of New Orleans. Following the Louisiana Purchase, Anglo-Americans began to pour into the city, but relations with the earlier French settlers were strained. By the 1830s, New Orleans was an officially divided city, with separate state governments for the Creoles and the Americans. There was a plan to build a canal along the wide stretch of land that divided the two quarters, but it was never implemented. Instead, the land designated for the canal became a neutral ground on which the Americans and the Creoles sometimes skirmished. To this day, the median down the center of Canal Street is known to most people in New Orleans as the "neutral ground".

The best way to gain an overview of the Central Business District is to go to the 31st floor of the **World Trade Center**. A glass elevator glides up the side of the building, and there are coin-operated telescopes situated at strategic points around the deck. With the whole city rolled out before you, the Mississippi River cuts a muddy

Joan of Arc statue

serpentine swath to the east. As you face the river, on the opposite bank and to your left is Algiers Point, *bête noire* of riverboat pilots. Turn your back to the river, and the French Quarter is to your right, with St Louis Cathedral looking as small as a dollhouse. Canal and Poydras streets begin just beneath your feet, Lake Pontchartrain is 11 miles ahead, and you're surrounded by the Central Business District. To your left about two miles away is the Garden District, and beyond it Audubon Park and the zoo, Uptown, and the University section. Before you leave the WTC, you might want to stop by the **Top of the Mart**, a revolving cocktail lounge on the 33rd floor. No food is served in the lounge, but there is a moderately priced cafeteria on the third floor.

When you leave the WTC, the mammoth building just in front of you is a casino with more bad luck than a gambler on a bad day. As we go to press, the ultimate fate of this land-based gambling den is still under debate. In 1995, the Rivergate Exhibition Center, which had stood on that site since the 1960s, was demolished to make way for a Harrah's casino. Harrah's opened a temporary casino in the Municipal Auditorium in Armstrong Park, which was to have closed when the Canal Street casino was completed. But, Harrah's went bankrupt, closed the temporary casino, and ceased work on the Canal Street building. Nothing has happened since.

On the neutral ground between the WTC and the ghost casino, is the bright golden **statue** of **Joan of Arc**. The statue's plaque reads:

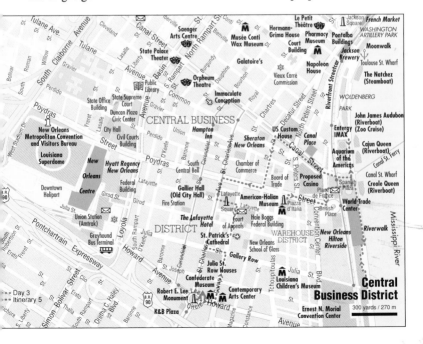

Creole Queen

"Maid of Orleans, 1412-1430. Gift from the people of France to the citizens of New Orleans." Charles de Gaulle presented the statue to the city in 1960. Joan of Arc reigns supreme in just one of four international plazas in this immediate vicinity, each of them commemorating New Orleans's European beginnings.

Nearby, almost in the front yard of the Hilton Hotel, **British Place** is a small circle of green grass with a large statue of Winston Churchill, and not a very flattering one at that.

At Tchoupitoulas Street, the third international plaza is **Piazza d'Italia**. This plaza, with its fountain and map of Italy, played a role in the opening scene of the film *The Big Easy*. In recent times it has got quite seedy-looking. For several years now there have been various announcements about hotel development around the Piazza; the fate of this once-lovely tribute to the city's hundreds of thousands of Italians is uncertain.

The most spectacular of the international plazas is **Spanish Plaza** (Plaza de España), between the World Trade Center and the Mississippi. At the Canal Street entrance to the plaza, which was a bicentennial gift to New Orleans from Spain, is a large equestrian statue of Bernardo de Galvez, who was governor of Louisiana from 1777 to 1785. The broad plaza is paved with mosaic tiles and has as its centerpiece a splendid fountain, embedded with Spanish coats of arms and shooting 50 feet (15m) of water.

The **Poydras Street Wharf** here is the boarding area for the **Creole Queen riverboat**, tickets for which are sold in kiosks around the plaza. As we went to press, the gambling riverboat **Flamingo** was docked here, but she's destined eventually for Shreveport on the Red River. This is also where Lundi Gras is held annually, a huge free-to-the-public party the Monday night before Mardi Gras (Fat Tuesday).

At one end of the plaza is the **Canal Street Ferry**, which crosses the river to Algiers on the west bank, and at the other is **River-walk**, an indoor mall with some 200 specialty shops and restau-rants, sidling along the river as far as the Ernest N. Morial Convention Center and Julia Street in the Warehouse District. On the lower level of Riverwalk there is an outpost of **Café du Monde**, and on the third level there is a food court. At the other end of the plaza, near the ferry entrance, **Le Moyne's Landing** is a seafood restaurant and oyster bar that sometimes features live jazz.

Riverwalk ramblings

The enormous modern building across Canal Street from the Canal Street Wharf is the **Aquarium of the Americas**, home to some 7,000 species of sea and river creatures. Admired by those who are not usually fish people, the aquarium has 60 separate displays in four major exhibit areas: the 132,000-gallon (500,000-liter) Caribbean Reef Environment, which has a transparent acrylic tunnel; the Amazon Rainforest Habitat, complete with high humidity and piranhas; the Mississippi River Habitat, which includes a Cajun shack; and the Gulf of Mexico Exhibit, with a 500,000-gallon (1,890,000-liter) tank. There are touch tanks, demonstrations, feedings and, in a separate wing, an IMAX theater. The aquarium is in the landscaped 17-acre (7ha) **Woldenberg Riverfront Park**, stretching along the Mississippi from Canal Street to Jackson Square in the French Quarter, a fine place for sunning, reading, river-watching, and building castles in the air. This is also the departure point for zoo cruises.

Walking away from the river up Canal Street you'll see **Canal Place**, an indoor pedestrian mall with many upscale shops. On the third level are four first-run cinemas, a food court, a health club and Southern Repertory, which mounts plays written by Southern playwrights.

Aquarium of the Americas

The entire 400 block of Canal Street is occupied by the **Old US Custom House**. The brooding gray structure, on the site of Fort St Louis, which guarded the 18th-century French city, was begun in 1848 but not completed till 1880. US Customs business is carried on in the colossal **Great Marble Hall**, which has been cited by the American Institute of Architects as one of the nation's finest late Greek Revival rooms. The hall measures 125 feet by 95 feet (38m by 29m), and the ceiling is 54 feet (16m) high. The skylight is supported by 14 white Corinthian columns, each with a matronly 4ft (120cm) waistline.

Another of the city's Greek Revival treasures is **Gallier Hall**, opposite Lafayette Square. Government offices are now housed in the Hall, which isn't open to the public. James Gallier Sr designed the building, which was to house administrative offices for the second municipality when the city was divided. When the city was consolidated in 1852, this became City Hall and remained so until municipal offices moved to their present Loyola Avenue location. Every Mardi Gras morning, the mayor stands on the steps of Gallier Hall and the Rex parade stops while the King of Carnival and the Mayor of the City exchange toasts.

Across Lafayette Square, the tall and slender gray structure is **St Patrick's Cathedral**. The Americans who poured into New Orleans in the 1800s felt that in St Louis Cathedral God spoke only in French; this lovely church was erected for Irish Catholic worshippers. Designed along the lines of York Minster in England, the cathedral was begun in about 1838 by James and Charles Dakin. Following a dispute between the Dakins and church trustees, James Gallier Sr was called in to finish the work. The three dramatic murals over the main altar were painted in 1840 by Leon Pomarede.

In the 1830s, this area was to the new American arrivals what the Place d'Armes was to the Creoles, and **Lafayette Square** was the Americans' foremost public place. The city's second oldest square, it was laid out in 1788. The park was at one time enclosed in a cast-iron fence, like Jackson Square, but the fence has long since disappeared. When the square was under development, it was intended that a large equestrian statue of the Spanish king be erected in its center. Instead, the statuary now in the square is of Henry Clay and of John McDonogh, a philanthropist who bequeathed funds for the city's public schools. This is not at all a good place to be after dark, alone or otherwise.

Statue of John McDonogh

The chic **Lafayette Hotel** is right next to the park, where **Mike's on the Avenue** is an upscale eatery much loved by locals. On the other hand, the all-night **Hummingbird Grill** a couple of blocks up St Charles is a greasy spoon whose customers run the gamut from swells to ne'er-do-wells.

Poydras Street is notable for its plethora of towering, streamlined office buildings. Not far from the **Civic Center**, the famous, stupendous

Superdome hunkers like a giant spaceship on Poydras Street. The Dome is home to the New Orleans Saints football team and host of

the annual Sugar Bowl college football game. More Super Bowl games have been played here than in any other city.

Lafayette Hotel

In addition to sports events, the Dome has been the arena of everything from Rolling Stones concerts to a Republican National Convention. It opened in 1975, cost upwards of $180 million, and is touted as the largest facility of its kind in the world. The statistics are mind-boggling. It encompasses a total land area of 52 acres (21ha) – the dome alone covers more than 9 acres (4ha) – and has parking for 5,000 cars and 250 buses. It rises to a height of 27 storys; the diameter of the dome is 680 feet (207m). You can learn much more about the Superdome on one of the daily guided tours.

The Superdome, New Orleans Centre, the Hyatt Regency Hotel, and Poydras Plaza form a veritable community along Poydras Street. The newest and most stylish kid on the block is the pretty pink **New Orleans Centre**, which is a high-rise complex of offices and shops. Macy's and Lord & Taylor are the best-known of its many stores. **Poydras Plaza**, of which the Hyatt Regency is a part, also contains offices and shops, and has been a fixture on this street for many years.

Superbowl fans in front of the Superdome

Lake Pontchartrain Tour

Reserve a car the previous day for this tour. Allow about two hours to drive without stopping along the Drive, but a much better idea is to turn the trip into an entire day's tour out of town.

To reach **Lakeshore Drive**, take I-10 East and exit at Downman Road, about 2 miles (3km) from the Interstate. Downman deadends at a sign pointing to Lakefront Airport and South Shore Marina. Turn left and follow Leon C. Simon Drive across the Seabrook Bridge. Keep to the right-hand lane because Lakeshore Drive swings to the right just over the bridge and there are no signs indicating that. (Note that Monday through Thursday Lakeshore Drive has two-way traffic, but Friday through Sunday it is one-way going west.)

The lakefront area is one of New Orleanians' favorite playgrounds. There are usually sailboats, Jet Skis and waterskiers, as well as folks patiently fishing from the amphitheater-like steps that lead to the lake. Though Lake Pontchartrain is only about 15 feet (5m) deep, it covers 610 square miles (1,580 sq km).

Until the 1920s and a massive 2,000-acre (800ha) landfill project, the lakefront consisted largely of fishing shacks balanced on pilings. The five-mile-long (8km) **Lakeshore Drive Park** is one of the results of the landfill. All along the drive there are picnic pavilions, concession stands, and plenty of parking bays. **Lakefront Airport**, which serves small corporate and private planes, will be on your right as you begin the Drive, and to your left, US Marine

Shrimp boat on the lake

Headquarters and a Naval Reserve Training Center. A little to the south of Lakeshore Drive, **Pontchartrain Park** is home to the **Joseph Bartolomew Golf Course**, one of the city's several public courses. At Franklin Avenue, the **Kiefer UNO Lakefront Arena** of the University of New Orleans is a major venue for top-name concerts and sports events. The pavilion on your left was built for the outdoor mass celebrated by Pope John Paul II on his 1987 visit.

Mardi Gras Fountain

The drive leads through Lake Terrace, a modern upscale neighborhood, and around Lake Terrace Parkway, a lovely place where lakefront residents enjoy jogging. As you cross over **Bayou St John**, which Bienville named in the 1700s for his patron saint, look to your left for a splendid view of the skyline beyond the dome of the Greek Orthodox Church. In this section of the drive you'll be at the northernmost part of City Park *(See Pick & Mix Tour 8, page 66).*

Marconi Boulevard is the western border of City Park, and just past it a concession stand called **Shelter No. 2** sells Sabrett's ("New York's famous") hot dogs, snacks and ice cream. There's also a "Tot Lot" playground, picnic area and rest rooms.

Next on your left is the **Mardi Gras Fountain**, around which plaques and crests honor all of the "krewes" (Carnival clubs), past and present. When it's turned on, the fountain spouts water in the Mardi Gras colors of green, gold and purple.

A big sign announcing **Joe's Crab Shack** also marks the end of Lakeshore Drive and the beginning of **West End Park**. Notice just behind the Crab Shack the turn-of-the-cen-

Joe's Crab Shack

tury **wooden lighthouse**, still very much in operation. Keep to your right for Roadway Drive West that leads out to **Breakwater Drive**,

Longue Vue House spiral staircase and (right) full moon over Lake Pontchartrain

from which there's a splendid view of the lake. The Point is a turn-around place at the end of the drive. North and South Roadway Drives embrace West End Park, where splendid oak trees arch over the street. North Roadway leads around the **New Orleans Municipal Yacht Harbor**, which is open to the public, and **Southern Yacht Club**, which is not. The Southern is the nation's second oldest yacht club. This area, awash with water-related concerns, seems light years away from downtown and the French Quarter.

South Roadway connects with the Old Hammond Highway across the 17th Street Canal to **Bucktown**, an ages-old fishing village. **R&O's Pizza**, **Sid-Mar's** and **Carmine's** are but three of the popular downscale seafood restaurants here beloved of New Orleanians.

Backtracking, drive to Pontchartrain Boulevard and turn right. Take the I-10 exit to Metairie Road. Turn right on Metairie Road and then left on Bamboo Road to reach **Longue Vue House and Gardens**. Longue Vue was the home of cotton broker Edgar Stern and his wife, Edith Rosenwald Stern, heiress to the Sears fortune. Now a museum of decorative arts, the 45-room mansion is surrounded by eight acres (3ha) of manicured gardens, including the Spanish Court, modeled after the 14th-century Generalife Gardens of the Alhambra in Spain.

Pizza by the lake

Not far away by car, **Metairie Cemetery** was a racetrack in the 1850s. The city's largest cemetery, and the most photographed, Metairie covers 150 acres (60ha) of landscaping, trees and lagoons. And of course, tombs – some 7,000 mausoleums, society tombs and monuments.

PICK & MIX

1. Mardi Gras Tour

Enjoy aspects of Mardi Gras all year round. Begin at the Old US Mint, 400 Esplanade Avenue, on the border of the Quarter.
See map on pages 18-19

Don't be fooled. Gazing on Carnival memorabilia doesn't come

Carnival capers on Canal Street

close to experiencing real, live Mardi Gras. But what the exhibits may do is whet your appetite so you'll come see it for yourself.

The **Old US Mint** on Esplanade Avenue, built in 1835 on the site of an old Spanish fort, was indeed a branch of the Federal mint until it was closed during the Civil War. Nowadays, it houses museums that are dedicated to two things for which the city is justifiably famous: music and Mardi Gras. The **Jazz Museum** traces the Crescent City's musical heritage (exhibits include native son Louis Armstrong's first horn), and across the hall is the **Mardi Gras Museum**.

This uses artists' drawings, dioramas, photographs and glittering costumes to demonstrate how Carnival works. There are also displays of sceptres and crowns, invitations to Carnival balls and some of the favors given at balls. A highlight of the museum is the life-size figure of Rex, King of Carnival, seated with his Queen in all their glittering glory presiding over the Rex 1928 Carnival ball.

Don't miss the Mardi Gras Indians display. Mardi Gras "Indians" are not Indians at all, but blacks who parade every year early on Mardi Gras morn and on St Joseph's Day. The custom dates from the 1800s, and may have begun in slavery days. The museum's exhibit is of a chief of the Wild Tchoupitoulas, decked out in an elaborate costume of sequins, feathers and plumes. There are no more intricate and eye-popping costumes than

Mardi Gras Museum exhibit

those of the Mardi Gras Indians, all carefully made by hand.

To reach **Arnaud's** restaurant from the Old US Mint, walk through the Quarter to Bienville Street. The restaurant is between Bourbon and Dauphine streets, and houses the **Germaine Wells Mardi Gras Museum** on the second floor. Germaine Cazenave Wells was the daughter of the gentleman who founded the restaurant in 1918, Count Arnaud Cazenave. ("Count" was an honorary title.) She was also queen of more Carnival balls than any other woman in New Orleans history. Between 1937 and 1968 she reigned over 22 of them, and she's buried in a copy of the shimmering gown she wore in 1954 as Queen of the Naiades ball. There are more bugle beads and rhinestones here than you can shake a sceptre at, in gowns, crowns and costumes worn by her pages. In addition to the Carnival regalia, there are Easter bonnets worn by Ms Wells, who initiated the carriage parades through the Quarter on Easter Sunday. Ms Wells died in the 1980s, and the parading tradition is now carried on by Bourbon Street entertainer Chris Owens. Sadly, open-topped limousines have replaced the horse-drawn carriages.

Queen of Carnival dresses

You'll find **Blaine Kern's Mardi Gras World** across the river in Algiers. Take the Canal Street Ferry for the breezy 10-minute crossing. You needn't worry about transportation in Algiers: a shuttle bus from Blaine Kern's meets all of the ferries. Blaine Kern's is the world's largest float-building firm. In the huge Algiers warehouses – called dens – artisans create the fantastic floats that sail through seas of people during Carnival. The giant faces and figures are made of papier-mâché, paint, imagination and magic. (Be sure to bring your camera.)

For Kern and his artisans, float-building is a year-round operation. As Carnival nears, the workforce increases from 60 or 70 to over 400 designers, artists, sculptors, carpenters and electricians. They design and decorate the floats for 40 of the 60 or so parading "krewes". There's a short video you can watch and a gift shop for Carnival-related memorabilia. Kern was once offered a job by Walt Disney, but chose to stay put because "Louisiana feeds me well." This Algiers native makes floats for other events, too, like Macy's Thanksgiving parade, but for him there's no place like home.

LaBranche building at night, Royal Street

2. Royal Street Tour

The section of Royal Street between Canal and Orleans streets can be walked in 10 minutes. But as it's a browser's paradise, there will be plenty of places you'll want to explore.
See map on pages 18-19

Royal Street is one of the Quarter's prettiest boulevards, overhung with balconies and lined with antique street lanterns. Formerly the location for several banks and financial institutions, this is now the street of expensive antique stores and art galleries. Money, now as then, is the keynote to Royal. If you have plenty to spare, this is the place to spend it. If you don't, the window-shopping here can be pleasant too.

The block between Canal and the uptown side of Iberville streets is not under the jurisdiction and preservation of the Vieux Carré Commission, which is why a McDonald's sits in this block and a Walgreens Drug Store is on the corner. This stroll along Royal Street begins on the downtown side of Iberville.

The Citizen's Bank is gone from the corner of Iberville and Royal, but its memory lingers on in the word "Dixie." In the 1830s, because the city was a mix of French Creoles and Americans, the bank printed banknotes in French as well as in English. Ten-dollar bills were printed on one side with *dix*, the French word for ten. New Orleans was flourishing at the time, and came to be known far and wide as the "land of the dixes" – a place where a lot of money could be made – and thus "Dixieland" was coined, almost literally. Alternatively, the name may come from the Mason-Dixon Line, the boundary between the northern and southern states. But since we're in the old money street of New Orleans, let's stick with the 10-dollar bill derivation.

Mr B's Bistro, at 201 Royal, is a member of the well-known

Brennan family of restaurants. The Mr B is Ralph Brennan, who operates the bistro with his sister, Cindy. There is a charcoal grill here, and you know you're nearing the restaurant when those wonderful aromas waft your way.

Across the street, the **Monteleone Hotel** (No. 214) has reigned since 1886. In the 1800s, a Sicilian bootmaker named Antonio Monteleone had a factory across the street from the little Commercial Hotel at Royal and Bienville streets. He dreamed of someday owning it, and in time he did. The luxury 16-story, 600-room Monteleone, the oldest and tallest hotel in the Quarter, is run by the fourth generation of Monteleones.

The **French Antique Shop** (No. 225) carries, among other treasures, fine chandeliers, and the neighboring **Hanson Art Gallery** (No. 229) has in its collection works by Peter Max, Liepke, Kline, Neiman and Musick.

Some of these antique stores are now operated by a third or fourth generation of the founders. Three

French Antique Shop

of them – **Moss** (No. 411), **Keil** (No. 325) and **Royal** (Nos. 307-309) – are operated by descendants of Hermina and Jacob Keil, who opened The Royal Company antique store in 1899. Billy Rau, proprietor of **M. S. Rau** (No. 630), is the grandson of Mendel and Fanny Rau, who first opened their doors in 1912. The oldest antique store on the street is Waldhorn, which celebrated its centennial in 1980. In 1997, Waldhorn was purchased by Adler & Son jewelers, and the store is now **Adler & Waldhorn**. Stephen A. Moses is a fourth-generation proprietor.

Hanson Art Gallery

The building occupied by Adler & Waldhorn (No. 343) was built around 1800 for Vincent Rillieux, a great-grandfather of Edgar Degas, the French Impressionist painter. The architect was Barthelemy Lafon, architect and surveyor during the late Spanish Colonial period. From 1820 to 1836 this was the Bank of the United States. At about that same time, the lovely pink building across the street, at No. 334, was the Bank of Louisiana. Now it's headquarters for the Vieux Carré police, and for the Vieux Carré Commission. **Café Beignet** is next door, a pleasant place to rest over gourmet snacks like pastries, sandwiches, salads and strong coffee; its patio is virtually in the side yard of the police station.

Another former bank now houses **Manheim Galleries** (Nos. 403-409). It was designed in 1820 by Benjamin Henry Latrobe, a noted architect who contributed to the US Capitol and designed the Bank of Pennsylvania in Philadelphia. The Louisiana State Bank was one of his last works. The bank's former directors' boardroom now houses one of the world's largest collections of jade. Manheim is the local agent for Boehm Birds, the delicate collectors' items designed by American potter Edward Marshall Boehm. Bernard Manheim established this gallery in 1910; his son Abe is the present proprietor.

Brennan's Restaurant (No. 417), which celebrated its 50th year in 1996, was the first Brennan family enterprise. In the mid-1970s, some members of the family split to begin founding other upmarket eateries. The first was Commander's Palace, in the Garden District, followed by Mr B's Bistro, the Palace Café, Bacco and the newest, Redfish Grill. Brennan's, famous for lavish breakfasts and a glorious courtyard, occupies a house that dates from 1795. It was the Banque de la Louisiane, and later the home of Paul Morphy, America's most famous chess player.

Nearby is the New Orleans branch of **Dyansen Gallery** (No. 433), which has one of the largest collections of works by Erte. And next to it, **James H. Cohen & Son** (No. 437) is a large, fascinating store that stocks antique weapons, swords, rare coins, Confederate currency and a world of other items, including some of Frederick Remington's bronco busters and a wooden Indian that guards the front door.

Dog optional

The white baroque building that occupies the entire 400 block across the street is the **Louisiana Supreme Court**. It was built around 1908 as the Civil Courts building, and served for a time as headquarters of the Wildlife & Fisheries Agency. As we went to press, renovation was under way for its new life. In the Oliver Stone film *JFK*, this building contained the offices of Jim Garrison, as played by Kevin Costner. Its front steps are often the stage for a variety of street performers.

In fact, during the day, when Royal Street is closed to motor traffic, itinerant musicians and other performers often take to the middle of the street to entertain passers-by. The quality of performance varies, of course, but most of them are quite good. There is an outstanding pony-tailed piano-player who rolls his upright around, parks it and sits down to play ragtime. Banjoists and guitarists are much in evidence.

The **Rib Room**, at the corner of Royal and St Louis, is the main dining room of the **Royal Orleans**, one of the city's finest hotels.

Ginja Jar

Built in 1960, it's on the site of a very famous hotel built here in the 1830s. It was the elegant St Louis Exchange Hotel, which was badly damaged by fire in 1916, and its remains razed. You can see a large picture of it in the lobby of the "Royal O."

Pause to peer in the window of **Le Petit Soldier Shop** (No. 528) and examine the faces of the miniature military figures. Among them you'll see Generals Lee and Grant, also Hitler, Churchill, Eisenhower and Stalin. The **Historic New Orleans Collection** (No. 533) is a repository for the private collection of Leila and Kemper Williams, one of the largest private collections of documents, paintings, maps, blueprints and artifacts in the nation. The library and research facilities are excellent. The ground floor **Williams Gallery**, with its changing exhibits of artworks pertaining to the city, is free. For a nominal fee you can take a tour of the historic house. Built in 1792 as the home of Jean François and Catherine Merieult, it was one of the few buildings to survive the 1794 fire.

Catherine Merieult apparently possessed something that Napoleon fervently desired – her hair. Anxious to secure a political alliance with Turkey, Bonaparte made repeated attempts to purchase Mme Merieult's mane of blonde hair, having learned that the sultan of Turkey required a blonde wig for one of his sultanas. Despite being offered a fortune in cash, and even a castle, Catherine stoutly rejected the emperor's requests.

Nahan Galleries (No. 540), across the street from a Dansk factory outlet, is the corporate headquarters for galleries in New York and Japan. Among the artists represented are Max Papart and Helen Finch. The **Ginja Jar** (No. 607) and **Ginja Jar Too** (No. 611) are charming shops with lovely hand-made dolls, doll carriages, antique walking sticks and a Santa's workshop of other things. The **Court of Two Sisters** (No. 613) is a restaurant that's famous for its beautiful courtyard. The house gets its name from two sisters who had a notions shop here in the late 1800s. The house that stood here originally was the home of Governor de Vaudreuil, who assumed governorship of the colony immediately after Bienville. His house was destroyed in the fire of 1788; the present one dates from the early 1800s.

The restaurant does a daily jazz brunch that tourists adore. More than 60 food items are on the huge menu: regional dishes such as jambalaya, shrimp creole, crawfish etouffée and gumbo, along with baked ham, barbecue ribs and roast beef, not to mention an enticing array of desserts. A strolling trio of jazz musicians entertains around the wishing well, the banana trees and tropical birds. Waiters here are well-practiced in the art of photo-taking, which is a fa-

Preserving traditional jazz

vorite brunchtime activity.

At No. 623, **Royal Blend** is a great place for quiches, croissant sandwiches, pastries and gourmet coffee. Entrance is through the carriageway, beyond which there is a lovely courtyard with umbrella tables. Dining is inside or al fresco.

These days, the **Old Town Praline Shop** (No. 627) turns out the best pralines in town. While munching on your pecan candy, walk out into the courtyard – a beauty. This is the house where, in 1860, the 17-year-old soprano sensation Adelina Patti stayed while performing at the French Opera House. Young Creole men of the day would hang around outside hoping to catch a glimpse of her, or to listen to her vocalizing.

The building at **640 Royal** goes under several aliases, being known variously as the LeMonnier House, the First Skyscraper, and 'Sieur George. It comes by all three names honestly. The house was built between 1795 and 1811 by noted architect Barthelemy Lafon for Dr Yves LeMonnier. The wall and balcony at the corner curve around an oval salon. You can see the initials "YLM" worked into the wrought iron on the balcony.

As for First Skyscraper, legend has it that the top floor was added in order to make sure this remained the tallest building in the French Quarter. Regarding 'Sieur George, that was the name of the title character in one of George Washington Cable's short stories, who occupies a rented room in this house. As in the case of Madame John's Legacy on Dumaine Street, in the story the character is fictitious, the house real. During the 19th century, Cable wrote caustic tales about the Creoles of New Orleans, often putting his characters in well-known locations.

Hardly a tourist attraction, the Royal Street A&P is one of three supermarkets in the area. A "supermarket" in the Quarter is not quite the same as a supermarket any place else. You won't find, for example, wide aisles, or sacks of dogfood big enough to feed 101 dalmatians. Things tend to be on a smaller scale. But the store is open 24 hours (there's an, umm, interesting crowd in here at three in the morning), except for the Monday night before Fat Tuesday. During the five-day Mardi Gras weekend, most businesses just try to dig in and endure.

(Just up St Peter Street, in the 700 block, **Preservation Hall** and its neighbor, **Pat O'Brien's**, are perhaps the city's two most fa-

Pat O'Brien's

mous establishments. Preservation Hall, in a former stable, presents authentic traditional jazz every night. Pat O'Brien's is an historic bar constructed round a stunning courtyard. It was built in 1791 and used for a century as a theater, before it became the bar where New Orleans's ubiquitous Hurricane – a cocktail of rum and passion fruit juice – was invented.)

Across from the A&P, the **LaBranche Buildings**, which date from 1840, are 11 separate three-story buildings standing shoulder to shoulder, from 708 Royal Street and wrapping around the corner to 639 St Peter. Eight of them face St Peter Street, one fronts on Royal Street, and two others overlook Pirate's Alley. The **Faulkner Book Store** is at 624 Pirate's Alley, and there's a cigar bar at the corner of Pirate's and Cabildo alleys. A Haagen-Dazs ice-cream parlor is at St Peter and Cabildo Alley, and the Royal Café occupies one of the best locations in town: it's at the corner of St Peter and Royal streets, and does a huge amount of business.

The LaBranche Buildings are swathed in elaborate cast iron, and where St Peter meets Royal is perhaps the most photographed corner in town. The buildings' cast iron was a lovely white until the late 1980s when someone had the bright idea of painting it grey.

Fleur de Paris

It's still pretty, but doesn't take your breath away as the white did. If you walk down St Peter Street toward the square, look up at the balconies on these buildings and you can see the different ways they were added. Wrought iron was introduced into Louisiana in about 1850; it became all the rage and was a later addition to many local buildings.

Going downriver on Royal (away from the CBD), you'll pass the traffic-stopping window of **Fleur de Paris** (No. 712), a very elegant ladies' shop. There are always stunning hats worn by the mannequins – the kind for which members of various royal families are known. In addition to exotic headgear, the shop carries an array of ladies' ready-to-wear, including wedding dresses, and also custom-makes hats and clothing. Be advised: it is all quite expensive.

Pirate's Alley and its twin, Père Antoine Alley, are passageways to Jackson Square. There are oftentimes artists at work along here, their wares displayed on the cast-iron fence that surrounds Cathedral Gardens.

Across Royal Street, on Orleans Street, is the **Orleans Ballroom**, now a part of the **Bourbon Orleans Hotel** (717 Orleans Street). In the early 19th century, this was one of the sites for "Quadroon Balls." The balls were held so that mulatto mothers could introduce their quadroon daughters to wealthy Creole gentlemen in hopes

Bergen Galleries

that an "alliance" would be formed. Mulattoes and quadroons were *gens de couleur libre*, "free people of color," many of whom sought refuge in New Orleans after the 1791 Santo Domingo slave uprising. When a man displayed an interest in a particular young woman, he and her mother would negotiate terms for an arrangement. Such arrangements usually meant that the Creole and the quadroon would openly live together in grand style. If the Creole subsequently married one of his own race, the arrangement ostensibly would come to an end, but in practice his quadroon mistress and any children they may have had would be financially taken care of for life. It was a European system of *placage* (veneer) that came over from the old country with the colonists.

Historians disagree (as historians are wont to do) as to the exact nature of the quadroon balls. Some say they were elegant affairs, others that they were little more than drunken brawls. In any case, this ballroom was bought in 1873 by the Catholic Sisters of the Holy Family, an order of black nuns, and became a convent and school. When the sisters moved to the suburbs in 1964, part of the old building was incorporated into the Bourbon Orleans Hotel, which now uses it for banquets and special events.

Speaking of hats, as we earlier were, **Bergen Galleries** (No. 730) is just ahead, perched at Père Antoine Alley. The proprietor, delightful Marguerita Bergen, is well known for her *chapeaux*. She is always beautifully "turned out," as the saying goes. Her gallery is one of the best places in town for Jazz Fest and Mardi Gras posters — almost any kind of poster, framed or unframed.

Blue Dog by Cajun artist George Rodrigue

In the gallery across Royal from Bergen, the alert-looking royal blue canine with the big yellow eyes staring out the window is **George Rodrigue's** trademark **Blue Dog**. The dog was drawn from life — Rodrigue used his own pup as a model when illustrating a children's book — and after that the Blue Dog took on a life of her own. The well-known Cajun artist has galleries from Louisiana to Germany and Japan.

50

Sign of the times

3. The Many Faces of Bourbon Street

Let's face it; Bourbon Street has a bad reputation. It's world-famous as a place where drunks stagger in and out of bawdy girlie shows and otherwise intelligent people behave like idiots. Does that happen? Oh, you bet. But Bourbon is a very mixed bag, as we shall discover. *See map on pages 18-19*

In the early mornings, Bourbon may still smell of bourbon, but it's quiet, except for the folks hosing down the sidewalks from the night before. It isn't until around noon that music begins a slow trickle into the streets. By mid-afternoon, the trickle has become a stream, and by nightfall a flood of sounds pours out of jazz clubs all along the street. You can hear most any kind of music, from R&B to Cajun to ragtime piano to gutbucket (that's lowdown, mean blues).

You don't even have to go inside to listen to it. The doors are always flung wide, and you can lean against a lamp-post and listen till the cows come home. Or till you get thirsty. And if you do go inside, you're not obliged to stay until you've finished your drink. Almost any place that serves mixed drinks also provides "go-cups,"

Welcome to Galatoire's

so you can take your libation with you while strolling along.

Standing in front of clubs all along the street, barkers keep up a steady spiel to lure customers in. They are as characteristic of the street as abandoned go-cups, those barkers that work the crowds like their "carnie" kin. They usually double as bouncers when the clientele gets too rowdy.

But Bourbon is more than a noisy carnival midway. For example, the elegant French Creole restaurant **Galatoire's** is at No. 209, a few doors down from a topless bar. Galatoire's was established in 1905, and is operated now by descendants of the founder. The long lines of well-dressed people you see in front are waiting for a table: the restaurant does not take reservations – and does not allow jeans or, heaven forbid, shorts. Many Orleanians consider this the finest

restaurant in town; others say it's a toss-up between Galatoire's and the excellent Commander's Palace in the Garden District. Galatoire's, however, is the acknowledged place to be on Friday afternoons.

The **Old Absinthe House**, at 240 Bourbon, a funky bar with football helmets hanging from the ceiling, is older than the **Old Absinthe Bar** (No. 400), which has hard-driving late-night blues and R&B. The House is a plain drinking bar. The two are loosely related: during Prohibition, while the House was closed down, someone broke in and virtually cleaned the place out. Sometime later the fixtures and everything turned up at No. 400, and the Bar was born. The House, built in 1805, is an *entresol* design: two stories with a mezzanine sandwiched between, usually used for storage and lit by handsome fanlights. The House and the Bar both claim to have been among the places Jean Lafitte and Andrew Jackson met to map out the 1815 Battle of New Orleans. So say the legends.

The **Royal Sonesta Hotel**, at No. 300, is as peaceful as Bourbon is rowdy. Not, however, if you've booked a balcony room overlooking "the street." You won't get a wink of sleep. The hotel has a splendid courtyard with fragrant orange trees, and there are balconies on the courtyard side, too. However, few people come to New Orleans to catch up on sleep. Just off the marble lobby, the sophisticated Mystick Den lounge is home court for the classy jazz pianist Ronnie Kole.

For many Mardi Gras veterans, Mardi Gras just isn't Mardi Gras unless you have a "balcony on Bourbon." After the krewes have paraded on Canal Street the hordes surge into the Quarter, primarily

Royal Sonesta Hotel

to Bourbon Street. All along the street balconies are stuffed full of people, most of them not entirely sober, who are engaged in tossing beads, doubloons and other trinkets into a carpet of screaming people below. (If you're in a hurry to get from point A to point B on Bourbon, you're better off detouring on Chartres Street, which is usually ever so slightly less congested.)

The majority of the topless-bottomless let-it-all-hang-out establishments are in the 300 and 500 blocks of Bourbon, but there are some respectable spots mixed in with the sleaze. The fairly touristy **Famous Door**, at No. 339, has been going strong since 1934, supplying dixieland and R&B. At 500, Bourbon Street legend **Chris Owens** provides a flashy Las Vegas-type show in her supper club. On Easter Sunday, Ms Owens heads up the Easter Parade, riding in a convertible and wearing a chic *chapeau*. The **Cajun Cabin** (No. 501) has an authentic Cajun chef and very good food, as well as ear-splitting music.

The Famous Door, established in 1934

The **Inn on Bourbon** (No. 541) is on the site of the French Opera House. A plaque on the side of the building recounts its glory and its tragedy. By all accounts, the French Opera House, built in 1859, was an elegant and essential part of the Creole social scene. Parents brought their young debutante daughters to the opera, as a way of presenting the girls to society.

Notice how the curb swerves inwards here: this was to accommodate the horse-drawn carriages that pulled up to let off ladies and gentlemen in their fancy dress. But it all came to a flaming end in 1919, when the opera house burned to the ground. If any attempts were made to rebuild it, they were obviously unsuccessful.

A bit farther down, the handsome galleried building between Orleans and St Ann streets is the **Bourbon Orleans Hotel**. The hotel lies on the site of the Orleans Theatre, built in 1817 by promoter and impresario John Davis, who was also instrumental in the opening of the French Opera House. This was also the site of the Orleans Ballroom, where many Quadroon Balls were held. *(See Pick & Mix 2 on page 49.)* It's possible to see the side of the ballroom from Royal and Orleans streets – look up to the right of the tall elegant portals of the hotel.

Continuing downriver on Bourbon Street, you're now approaching a predominantly gay section of the Quarter. In the 800 block, the **Bourbon Pub**, No. 801, and its glitzy upstairs **Parade Disco**, is a popular gay bar, and so is **Oz**, right across the street at No. 800.

Lafitte's Blacksmith's Shop

A block farther, at No. 901, **Café Lafitte in Exile** (not to be confused with Lafitte's Blacksmith Shop in the next block) is virtually a part of the landscape; the well-known gay bar has been on the scene since 1952.

The Quarter has a sizable gay population, and this area is lively indeed on Gay Pride Day and "Southern Decadence Day" (which some still call Labor Day). There are balconies all along the street, and they are jam-packed during Mardi Gras. There are two or three gay krewes that parade around here during Mardi Gras, and Burgundy Street at St Ann is the venue for the annual gay costume contest on Fat Tuesday. An eye-opening event if ever there was one.

Gay pride on Bourbon

The **Washing Well Laundryteria**, No. 841, is pretty much what its name proclaims – and a reminder that the Quarter is residential, as well as a tourist mecca. The Washing Well has been around for a while. It appeared with Robert Redford in the 1966 film *This Property is Condemned*: Redford hurried past it in hot pursuit of Natalie Wood. The Laundryteria is getting some stiff competition from nearby **Hula Mae's Tropic Wash & Beach Café** (840 N. Rampart Street). It's open 24 hours, and you can not only do laundry but get a sandwich, play the jukebox, watch TV, fax a letter, mail a package and surf the Internet. Hula Mae's even has a van that will pick up you and/or your laundry, and deliver you and/or it back home again.

You're now approaching what is known locally as "the quiet end of Bourbon." **Lafitte's Blacksmith Shop**, No. 941, according to the legend, was a front for the nefarious activities (possibly smuggling and/or slave trading) of the brothers Jean and Pierre Lafitte. It's very easy to imagine this ramshackle little cottage as a blacksmith shop, and certainly it's old enough to fit the Lafittes' period in history. Ownership records for the house date back to 1772, and the house is of brick-between-posts design, a kind of construction used by the early settlers. Be all that as it may, this has been a neighborhood bar for ages, especially favored by artists and writers. An ambience of "Old New Orleans" oozes out of every crack, just as at the Napoleon House.

Across from Lafitte's, the **Clover Grill**, No. 900, is a 24-hour grill with good burgers and breakfasts. Its sibling is the **Poppy Grill**, also open 24 hours, on St Peter Street across from Preservation Hall.

Across St Philip Street, the **Lafitte Guest House**, No. 1001, was built in 1849 as a private residence. The

Number 1209 Bourbon Street

downstairs parlor is a marvel of Victoriana, with plush red sofas and fringed lampshades. The hotel claims a resident ghost in room 40, and believes she was the mistress of the house.

Before packing it in, walk a block farther to take a look at the houses at Nos. 1121 and 1209. Both are private residences, not open to the public, but they're delightful just seen from the street.

The tomb of Marie Laveau, voodoo queen

4. Magic Cemetery Walking Tour

The city's above-ground cemeteries fascinate visitors, but it's best to view them as part of an organized tour.

New Orleans's old cemeteries are often called "Cities of the Dead," because the tombs look for all the world like miniature white-washed houses in a landscaped subdivision. Pathways wind around small, crumbling brick "step tombs" – the earliest design – and more elaborate mausoleums and monuments. Some are tiny versions of court houses, banks and the sort of mansions you find in the Garden District. Many are surrounded by ornate cast-iron fences and garnished with frilly grills. The largest and most spectacular tombs are those of the city's many benevolent societies.

Burials below ground were impossible in the days before pumping stations. The French Creoles learned some hard lessons very fast, for instance that much of the Crescent City is below sea level, and graves that were dug in the ground rapidly filled with water.

Ready for a tour

So one reason for above-ground burials was practical. Another was that the French and Spanish Creoles loved to emulate fashions in Europe, where above-ground burials, at least for the affluent, were customary.

In the early 1830s, when the noted architect J.N.B. dePouilly came to New Orleans from Paris, he brought with him sketches he'd made of the Père Lachaise cemetery. DePouilly designed many of the monuments and mausoleums in St Louis Cemeteries No. 2 and No. 3. But the city's oldest surviving cemetery is St Louis No. 1, on Basin Street near the Quarter. It was established in 1789, the year after the great fire and an ensuing epidemic of yellow fever that took hundreds of lives.

Regrettably, New Orleans's older cemeteries can be extremely dangerous places. Muggings are not at all uncommon, and we urge you to tour the cemeteries only with an organized group. Besides ensuring your safety, your guide will be able to fill you in on much fascinating history.

Magic Walking Tours (tel: 588 9693) conducts guided walks of St Louis No. 1 daily at 10.30am and 1.15pm. The tour is good value for money and lasts about two hours. A guide meets the group at a tiny bar at 622 Pirate's Alley, at the corner of Cabildo Alley. The route to the cemetery is via Orleans Street to North Rampart Street, then over to Basin Street and the cemetery entrance at St Louis Street.

You'll find St Louis No. 1 is surrounded by a high wall, following a centuries-old Spanish custom. Within the wall itself are vaults, about 12ft (4m) high and 9ft (3m) wide, and called "ovens" because they resemble bakers' ovens. These were used for multiple burials, often by indigent families who were unable to afford individual, private tombs.

As a rule, the tombs in St Louis No. 1 are not quite as ornate as those in the later cemeteries, but this site is the final resting place for many prominent early Orleanians. Among them is **Etienne de Bore**, the city's first mayor and the man who revolutionized an industry by discovering how to granulate sugar. Others include **Paul Morphy**, who was world chess champion at age 21; **Homer Plessy**, whose 1892 challenge to Jim Crow segregation laws resulted in the 1896 US Supreme Court decision Plessy vs Ferguson establishing "separate but equal" legislation for blacks; **Blaise Cenas**, the first US Postmaster in New Orleans; and the two wives of William C.C. Clairborne, the first American governor of Louisiana, whose tombs bear remarkably similar inscriptions.

The putative tomb of the city's most infamous voodoo queen, **Marie Laveau**, wears a bronze historical plaque and is usually adorned by various voodoo charms. The priestess *may* be buried here, or the person interred may be her daughter, who was also called Marie Laveau.

If you opt for the tour, you'd be wise to take along some bottled water and to wear a straw hat; the only shade in the cemetery is in

Déjà Vu

the shadow of somebody's tomb. At the end, the guide escorts the group back into the Quarter, breaking up across from **Bayona**, a tiny restaurant at 430 Bayona. If refreshment is required, **May Baily's** is the cocktail lounge of the Dauphine Orleans hotel (415 Dauphine); and **Déjà Vu** (400 Dauphine) is a good 24-hour grill.

The building that begat the Warehouse District

5. Warehouse District Tour

This part of the Central Business District (CBD), with its renovated warehouses now housing art galleries, restaurants and apartments, can be toured in about an hour and a half, depending on the stops you make.

The Warehouse District is a pocket of the CBD that gradually took on a life of its own. Up until around the 1970s, this was indeed a district of warehouses, many of them abandoned. The renaissance that began with the Contemporary Arts Center developed into a major arena for galleries, and Julia Street, from Canal Street to Convention Center Boulevard, was transformed into "Gallery Row." The beautification of the area began in earnest following the World's Fair in 1984, when developers began converting empty warehouses into sleek condominiums.

We'll begin this tour at **Lee Circle**, where Howard Avenue intersects St Charles Avenue, and end at Julia Street and St Charles Avenue. The statue of **Robert E. Lee** sits atop a 60-foot (18m) fluted marble Doric column, and faces north. This is about the only

Lee Circle

place in town where locals can identify a compass point. Lee died in 1870 at the height of Reconstruction; the statue was not unveiled until 1884. Among those present at the dedication were Jefferson Davis, Lee's daughters Mildred and Mary, and P.G.T. Beauregard, the Creole New Orleanian who ordered the first shot of the War Between the States to be fired at Fort Sumter, South Carolina.

58

Across the street from Lee Circle is **K&B Plaza**. Displayed in the indoor-outdoor sculpture garden, the **Virlane Collection** includes important works by European and American contemporary artists. The focal point of the exhibition is the large granite *Mississippi River*, sculpted by the late Isamu Noguchi.

A block away, the Contemporary Arts Center and the Confederate Museum face each other across Camp Street. The **Confederate Museum** (No. 929), in a picturesque old building, was dedicated in 1891. The large collection includes part of Lee's silver service, personal effects of Jefferson Davis (donated by his widow), battle flags, paintings, weapons and documents.

K&B Plaza

The **Contemporary Arts Center** (No. 900) owes its life, so to speak, to the K&B Corporation. In 1974, some starving contemporary artists were looking for a place to display their work. K&B (which has a chain of local pharmacies) donated one of their abandoned warehouses and in 1976, following extensive renovations, the CAC was born. The 10,000 square foot (930 sq m) building has several galleries and two theaters, in which the avant-garde and the outrageous are often performed. The CAC is the centerpiece of the annual October Arts for Art's Sake festival, which celebrates the fall gallery openings with great enthusiasm.

Julia Street, a block and a half toward Canal Street, is known now as **Gallery Row**, stretching from St Charles Avenue to Convention Center Boulevard. As French Quarter rents went up, and the Warehouse District began to develop, many contemporary art galleries moved to this area. Gallery owners from other parts of the US have also gravitated to the area, with an eagerness that led to one magazine describing the Warehouse District as "the SoHo of the South" (after New York's arty district).

In the early 1830s, the street was called Julia Street Row, and until the Civil War was one of the most fashionable addresses in town. The block between Camp Street and St Charles Avenue was called the Thirteen Sisters, referring to a row of 13 elegant townhouses. The renovation of the Warehouse District was led by the Preservation Resource Center, which continues its efforts to preserve and protect historic neighborhoods. From time to time the PRC does guided architectural tours.

There's a good selection of eating options in this area. On the upscale side, **Emeril's** is at 800 Tchoupitoulas Street and **Mike's on the Avenue** is in the Lafayette Hotel, a block and a half toward Canal Street, at 600 St Charles Avenue. On the other hand, the **Hummingbird Grill** (804 St Charles Avenue) is a greasy spoon under a flophouse, but the food is good and eminently affordable.

6. Streetcar Tour up St Charles Avenue

Streetcar sightseeing

This tour can be combined with the Garden District Tour, beginning at carstop 16 on St Charles Avenue; with the Warehouse District Tour; or all on its own, in which case you'd board the streetcar at Canal and Carondelet streets in the CBD. This can be a "sit down" tour all the way or, if you've purchased a Visitour pass you can get on and off the streetcar as the spirit moves you. In any case, the tour ends at Camellia Grill on South Carrollton Avenue.

The development of New Orleans followed the Mississippi River uptown: the farther you go on St Charles Avenue, the newer the houses become. The avenue is still lined with so many handsome mansions, however, it is not humanly possible to see them all in one trip, no matter how much head-swiveling you do.

The architects who worked upriver of the Quarter were for the most part Yankees, Irish and Englishmen. Remember, this was the American Sector; the developments upriver were the result of Creoles snubbing the American newcomers. Unlike the French Quarter homes with their hidden courtyards, houses built in this area are surrounded by splendid gardens, as if the Americans were green-thumbing their noses at the Creoles.

At the corner of St Charles and Fourth Street, the **Grima House**

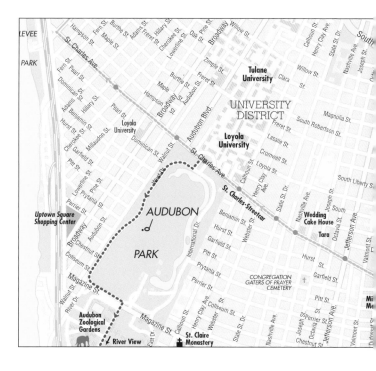

(1604 Fourth) seems almost fragile, despite its size (and the fact that it's been here for more than 100 years). Neither the architect nor the exact year of construction is known, but one Alfred Grima bought and restored it in the 1890s. Some historians think the house was built around 1850.

Columns Hotel

Christ Church Cathedral, the Fourth Episcopal Cathedral of New Orleans, is a wonderful Gothic structure, designed by New York architect Lawrence Valk and built in about 1887. Organ recitals are often held here on Sunday afternoon.

At 3811 St Charles, the **Columns Hotel,** named for its prominent architectural features, was built in the 1890s and is now a guest house. The interior staircase and stained glass window are magnificent; the Victorian Lounge is a favorite local watering hole. Interiors for the Louis Malle film *Pretty Baby* were shot here. In the next block, across the street, the **Rayne Memorial Methodist Church**, a brick church with a tall belfry, was built in about 1875.

Sacred Heart Academy, at No. 4521, easily identified by the words "Sacre Coeur" worked into the ironwork above the gate, is

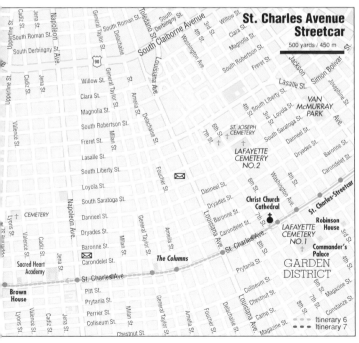

St. Charles Avenue Streetcar

500 yards / 450 m

VAN McMURRAY PARK

ST. JOSEPH CEMETERY

LAFAYETTE CEMETERY NO.2

Christ Church Cathedral

St. Charles Streetcar

Robinson House

LAFAYETTE CEMETERY NO.1

Commander's Palace

GARDEN DISTRICT

The Columns

St. Charles Ave

Sacred Heart Academy

Brown House

CEMETERY

--- Itinerary 6
--- Itinerary 7

A desirable streetcar

a very exclusive private school for Catholic girls. It was built around the turn of the century. Two blocks farther along St Charles, the exotic **Brown House** at No. 4717, embellished with Syrian arches and a perfectly manicured lawn, was completed in about 1905. The handsome mansion at No. 5005 was built in 1868 as a private home; it's now the headquarters of the exclusive women's social organization, the **Orleans Club**.

One of the few houses in this area that's open to the public is No. 5120, the **Milton H. Latter Memorial Library**, a branch of the New Orleans Public Library. It was built in 1907 and later was the home of Marguerite Clark, a stage and silent film star who, in her day, rivalled Mary Pickford in popularity.

Some Orleanians may tell you that *Gone with the Wind* was filmed in New Orleans, because there's a house call Tara on St Charles Avenue. Don't believe them. The film was shot on the back lot of a Hollywood movie studio. The St Charles Avenue **Tara**, at No. 5705, is an exact copy of the back lot Tara, and attracts its fair share of Scarlett O'Hara fans.

Wedding Cake House

A local tour guide is said to have christened the house at nearby No. 5809 "**The Wedding Cake House**" and the appellation has stuck. And for obvious reasons.

The South's largest Catholic university

Audubon Park stretches from 6300 to 6900 St Charles Avenue. Across from it, sitting cheek by jowl, are the lovely campuses of Loyola University and Tulane University. **Loyola**, the South's largest Catholic university, is the result of an early 19th-century merger of Loyola College and the Jesuits' College of the Immaculate Conception, which was established on Baronne Street in 1840. The university moved to its St Charles Avenue home in 1911. The campus, which includes the Holy Name of

62

Jesus Church, is lined with redbrick and terra-cotta buildings in the Gothic-Tudor style.

Tulane, renowned for its schools of law and medicine, was established by a group of doctors in 1834 as the Medical College of Louisiana. The college was originally located in what is now University Place in the Central Business District. In 1884 the school was endowed by Paul Tulane as a private university, and moved to its present location. The **Tilton Library**'s excellent research facilities include the New Orleans Jazz Archives and the Middle American Research Institute, which has extensive collections of pre-Columbian art.

Blossoms everywhere

St Charles Avenue ends at the uptown great bend in the river. The streetcar turns right on Carrollton Avenue and continues to the end of the line, Palmer Park. The **Riverbend levee** is a favorite place for walking, jogging, kite-flying or just lazing around.

In the 1830s this area was the resort town of **Carrollton**. The New Orleans & Carrollton Railroad (now the St Charles Streetcar) connected the resort to New Orleans, and people traveled out here to enjoy the racetrack, the beer, the botanical gardens and the hotel. Carrollton was incorporated into the city in 1843.

The first stop after the streetcar turns onto Carrollton Avenue is across from the **Camellia Grill**, a counter-service-only diner with white linen napkins and a maitre d' to see you to your stool. The burgers are great; so are the waffles and banana cream pie.

Carrollton flower shop

Audubon Park

7. Audubon Park and Zoo Tour

This tour can be combined with the Streetcar Tour, if the Garden District Tour is done separately. Plan to spend a full afternoon leisurely enjoying Audubon and the animals.

There are two equally attractive ways to get to and from the zoo. You can take a round-trip **Zoo Cruise** on the *John James Audubon* from the Aquarium of the Americas. (Buy a combination ticket that includes the cruise both ways and zoo admission.) Alternatively, take the streetcar up to Audubon Park and either stroll through the park to the zoo entrance or board the free Friends of the Zoo shuttle (it boards on St Charles in front of Loyola University), and then make the return trip downriver on the *John James Audubon*.

Audubon Park covers 340 lush acres (140 ha) between St Charles Avenue and the Mississippi. In the 1700s, this land was part of the Foucher and de Bore sugar plantations. Etienne de Bore was the sugar-grower who, in 1795, revolutionized the industry when he hit upon a method of granulating sugar for commercial production. In 1871, the city bought the land from speculators and created Upper City Park.

Around the turn of the century the name was changed to honor John James Audubon, the naturalist who spent a fair amount of time in Louisiana, in New Orleans and St Francisville, while working on his famous series *Birds of America*. Audubon Park was designed in part by Frederick Law Olmsted, the landscape architect who designed New York's Central Park. New Orleans's first world's fair took place here in 1884-85, when a 31-acre (12 ha) exhibition building sprawled over the site of the present 18-hole golf course. Unfortunately, not a trace of it remains.

The park is splendidly beautiful, shaded by ancient, gnarled oak trees wearing long grey beards of Spanish moss. Enormous, twisted boughs lean down to the ground, and big, thick roots push up through the earth. There are lagoons and duck ponds sprinkled around the park. Students from the universities are often seen here, studying, jogging or loafing.

The park was once a plantation

If you opt not to take the shuttle to the zoo, to the right of the main St Charles Avenue entrance a macadam path strings through the golf course and leads beneath Oak Alley to the zoo entrance. It's about a half-hour walk from the avenue. A somewhat longer route, to the left of the main entrance, has 18 exercise stations along the way.

In addition to the golf course, there are 10 unlighted outdoor tennis courts (at Tchoupitoulas Street) and Cascade Stables (near the zoo), which offer guided trail rides through the park.

Bearing up well

Audubon Zoological Gardens lies toward the river. It's a great zoo, with more than 1,800 animals lolling around natural habitats. Among them are an Australian domain, a tropical bird house, a sea lion pool, where feeding time occasions a great deal of barking and flapping about, an African savannah (where you can board the Mombasa tram to ride through parts of the zoo), and a Louisiana swamp exhibit, where 'gators bask on a bayou, looking disturbingly hungry. And speaking of which, there is a Cajun café here, dishing up huge helpings of jambalaya, red beans and rice, and hot dogs. This is also the venue for the annual Swamp Fest, a lively event with Cajun music, food and dancing.

Behind the zoo and across the tracks of the Public Belt Railroad, the **River View** area has sports fields and picnic grounds. The dock for the *John James Audubon* riverboat is straight ahead.

There is a third alternative for the trip up or downriver. The Magazine Street bus stops right in front of the zoo, which is at 6500 Magazine Street, and you can take it all the way to Canal Street.

Cooling off in City Park

8. City Park and Environs Tour

You could easily while away a full day here; at the very least allow a half-day for this tour. If you plan to take advantage of some of the sports facilities, you'll want to stretch that half-day to several days.

This beautiful 1,500-acre (600ha) park is one of the largest urban parks in the country. By now you have probably guessed that this, like other parks, sprawls over former sugar plantations. Public records note that this area was part of the French land grant that was awarded in 1718, the year New Orleans was founded.

As with Audubon Park, nature richly endowed City Park with oak trees and subtropical plants. There are several members of the Louisiana Live Oak Society here, an exclusive club whose members are strong, silent types, though quite leafy. The **John McDonogh Oak**, named for the benefactor of New Orleans's public schools, is believed to be an old gentleman of around 1,000 years. (This famous tree is near City Park Avenue, across Metairie Bayou from the Casino Building.)

Esplanade Avenue leads from the lower border of the Quarter and deadends at City Park Avenue. A large **equestrian statue** of General Pierre Gustav Toutant Beauregard guards the City Park Avenue entrance.

The **New Orleans Museum of Art**, approached via Lelong Drive, is in a lovely white neoclassical building that dates from 1911. NOMA, as it's called locally, has a $200 million collection that includes in its Impressionist section a portrait by Edgar Degas of Estelle Musson valued at $15 million. In 1872, Degas lived for several months with relatives in a house nearby, at 2306 Esplanade, that is now a bed-and-breakfast inn. The museum's collection includes pre-Columbian art, European masterpieces from the 17th,

18th and 19th centuries, American and European contemporary art, Louisiana artworks and furniture, and African and Asian artworks. There is a lovely collection of Carl Fabergé eggs, which he created for the Romanovs, and a 6,000-picture photography exhibit. The museum has a large gift shop, and a lunch room, which is a very pleasant place for a libation.

Near the museum, the **Dueling Oaks** are majestic trees where, it is said, hot-blooded Creoles dueled each other to the death, often over the hand of a southern belle.

Much activity takes place in City Park. There are golf courses and a 100-tee double-decker driving range; a lighted 39-court tennis center; diamonds for baseball and softball; and eight miles (5 km) of lagoons for canoeing and fishing. The **Casino Building** on Dreyfous Avenue, west of

Museum of Art

NOMA, has no casino but is the place to get fishing permits and to rent canoes and pedalboats for lazing on the lagoons with the swans. You can also buy ice-cream cones and snacks in the casino.

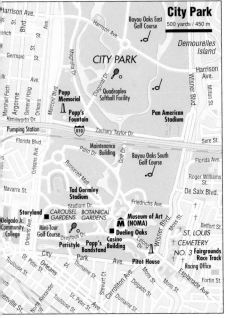

Adjacent to the casino is the **Botanical Garden**, with its lovely conservatory and parterre. Not far away, **Popp's Bandstand** does outdoor concerts. Not much farther, outdoor theater is sometimes performed in the 1907 **Peristyle**.

Storyland children's park is a great place for little ones, with its Mother Goose characters, Puppet Theater and story-telling times. In the very pretty **Carousel Gardens**, there's a small ferris wheel, a roller-coaster, antique cars and, best of

Pitot House on Bayou St John

all, a wooden turn-of-the-century **carousel**. It won't mean much to the kids, but in 1989 the carousel was put on the National Register of Historic Places.

There's also a **miniature train**, the *PGT Beauregard*, that scoots between Storyland and Carousel Gardens. For sports fans, the golf courses are in the northern section of the park, and there are several of them, all with 18 holes.

Cruising on the carousel

From late November until New Year's, during Celebration in the Oaks, City Park's trees are strung with hundreds of thousand of twinkling lights, and every night cars are lined up to drive through it. This is when City Park really comes into its own.

Before leaving this area, you should try to visit the extremely lovely, historic **Pitot House**, at 1440 Moss Street, which sits on **Bayou St John**, across City Park Avenue from the park. This is one of the oldest houses still on its feet in all of New Orleans.

The house dates from around 1799, and when New Orleans mayor James Pitot bought it in 1810 the house was considered a country home. It is now the property of the Louisiana Landmarks Society, which moved the house from 1370 Moss Street to its present location on the bayou. It has been lovingly restored, and is furnished with period furnishings. The Pitot House is open in the daytime Wednesday through Saturday.

Shopping

The city's largest shopping area is the French Quarter, one square mile of quaint little buildings that house clothing stores, jewelry shops, candy stores, shoe shops, record stores, shops for masks, make-believe and magic. The **Jax Brewery** (620 Decatur Street), an erstwhile brewery, and its cousin **The Millhouse** (600 Decatur Street) are filled with boutiques and food courts. The Jackson Brewery's third mall is called the **Marketplace** (414 St Peter Street).

The **French Market** (St Ann Street downriver to Barracks Street) has souvenir shops and open-air cafés. The old **Farmers' Market**, from Governor Nicholls Street to Barracks Street, has row after row of bins piled with fresh produce. There's a flea market in this part of the market where you can find Quarterites' cast-offs, records, books, tee-shirts, handcrafted jewelry and sundry junque.

In the CBD, **Canal Place** (333 Canal Street) is a tiny, upscale mall with good tenants like Saks Fifth Avenue, Gucci, Laura Ashley, the Pottery Barn, Brooks Brothers and Williams-Sonoma.

Up near the Superdome, **New Orleans Centre** (1400 Poydras Street), anchored by Macy's and Lord & Taylor, has a slew of chain shops and bookstores. **Riverwalk** (Spanish Plaza at Poydras Street) has 200 specialty shops and restaurants. In **Riverbend**, where the streetcar turns off St Charles

French Market

Avenue onto Carrollton, there are several worthy shops. **Magazine Street**, which stretches six miles (10 km) from the CBD to the Audubon Zoo, is row after row of antique stores, galleries, boutiques and bookstores.

Macon Riddle's company **Let's Go Antiquing** (tel: 899-3027) is designed to assist visiting shoppers to find what they're seeking, with minimal wear and tear on the nerves. Ms Riddle knows the shopping scene from A to Z. The **Louisiana Tax-Free Shopping** program, a boon for international visitors, is the only such program in the country. Here's how it works: look for a shop that displays the LTFS logo. When you make a purchase, pay the full price, including 9 per cent sales tax, and get a voucher for a tax refund. When you're departing, go to the Tax-Free Shopping office at New Orleans Inter-

Dolls all in a row

national Airport. Show them your passport, your ongoing ticket, and the voucher. Refunds of up to $500 will be made on the spot; for amounts more than that, a check will be mailed to the address of your choice.

Visitors almost always take home a box or two of pralines (those sweet, sweet concoctions of butter, sugar and pecans). Several stores have packaged New Orleans food to go. Carnival masks, Mardi Gras posters and Jazz Fest posters are favorite souvenirs, as are cans of Café du Monde coffee. It's hard to go wrong with jazz records and CDs made by local musicians.

Antique Stores

The list of New Orleans antique stores is long and distinguished. On Royal Street, go to the **French Antique Shop** (No. 225) for exquisite chandeliers, 18th and 19th century French furnishings, porcelains and bronze statues. **Keil's Antiques** (325 Royal) specializes in French and English antiques, chandeliers and gold-leaf mirrors. **Dixon & Dixon** (Nos. 237 and 301) has 20,000 square feet (1850 sq m) of space for showcasing antiques, estate jewelry and European oils from the 17th, 18th and 19th centuries.

Lucullus Antiques

M. S. Rau (No. 630) focuses on American antiques, jewelry, silver, porcelain and music boxes. **Royal Antiques** (Nos. 307-309) has 18th- and 19th-century country French and English furnishings, and brass and copper accessories. **Adler & Waldhorn** (No. 343), formerly Waldhorn Co, showcases antique American and English jewelry, 18th- and 19th-century English furniture, porcelain and silver.

Manheim (No. 403), the street's oldest store (since 1880) has not only 18th- and 19th-century English and French furniture, but also one of the world's largest and most beautiful collections of jade.

On Chartres Street: **Lucullus** (No. 610) is renowned for antique cookware, china, furnishings and objets d'art.

On Magazine Street: **French Collectibles** (No. 3424) sells 18th- and 19th-century French, Italian and English antiques and accessories. **Blackmoor** (Nos. 3433 and 324 Chartres) focuses on Chinese and English porcelain. **Charbonnet & Charbonnet** (No. 2929), which has a cabinet-making shop on the premises, has wonderful Southern country antiques.

Books

Faulkner House Books (624 Pirate's Alley) has a good selection of regional books. **Beckham's** (228 Decatur Street) and its sibling **Librairie** (823 Chartres Street) are both rather wonderfully Dickensian, with shelves full of used books. Also locally owned, **DeVille Books and Prints** (344 Carondelet Street, with an outlet at the New Orleans Centre) has a good selection of regional books, prints, and a framing shop.

The big guy on the block, **BookStar** (414 St Peter Street) is a cavernous store, operated by **Barnes & Noble**. (Speaking of which, the big cheese itself, Barnes & Noble, has opened a store in suburban Metairie – 3721 Veterans Memorial Boulevard, Metairie; tel: 455-4929 – with 32,000 square feet (3,000 sq m) and Starbucks coffee to boot.)

Nearer to town in the Garden District, the **Garden District Book Shop** (The Rink, 2727 Prytania) is the venue for Anne Rice's local booksigning sessions. On Magazine Street, the **Children's Hour Book Emporium** (3308 Magazine Street) is a large, bright store that carries books and games, and has special programs for kids. **Beaucoup Books** (5414 Magazine) stocks new issues, travel books and foreign language books.

Food to Go

In the French Quarter, the retail outlet of the **Louisiana School of Cooking** (Jax Brewery, 620 Decatur Street) has packages of red beans and rice, packaged pecans (in season), Cajun spices, beignet mix and cookbooks. **Gumbo Ya-Ya** (219 Bourbon Street) and **Creole Delicacies** (523 St Ann Street) both have gift packages of pralines, fudge and Cajun spices. At **Aunt**

Get your Cajun spices here

Sally's Praline Shop (810 Decatur Street) you can watch them make the pralines, then buy boxes to take home. At the **Old Town Praline Shop** (627 Royal Street) you don't get to watch the fixing,

but you can buy boxes to go, and the pralines themselves can't be beat.

Uptown, **Battistella's Seafood, Inc** (910 Touro Street) ships alligator meat, oysters, softshell crabs and shrimp, to name but a few. At the airport, **Bayou to Go** (Concourse C) has fresh Louisiana sea creatures, packaged and ready to travel on the plane with you.

Masks and Mardi Gras

In the Quarter, **Rumors** (513 and 319 Royal Street) has a crew of about 100 people making the fanciful besequined, feathery and leathery masks. At the **Little Shop of Fantasy** (523 Dumaine Street), Mike Stark makes wildly exotic creations. If you want to go the whole distance, the **Mardi Gras Center**, 831 Chartres Street, has costumes, full-face masks and theatrical makeup.

Mostly Mardi Gras (Jax Brewery, 620 Decatur Street) has a small but delightful selection of masks. **Masks & Make Believe** (Riverwalk) has everything from small ceramic decorative masks to full-fledged feathery creations.

Records and CDs

In the French Quarter, the **GHB Jazz Foundation** (61 French Market Place) is chock-full of dixieland, traditional jazz and R&B records, CDs and tapes. **Louisiana Music Factory** (225 N. Peter Street) zooms in on zydeco, Cajun and R&B. **Record Ron** (407 and 1129 Decatur Street) stocks Cajun, zydeco, rock and country, with a good inventory of local and international artists.

Louisiana Crafts

In the Quarter, **Crafty Louisianian** (813 Royal Street) has an eclectic collection of Cajun cornstalk dolls, Mississippi mud sculptures, palmetto baskets and handcarved wooden figures. **Coghlan Galleries** (710 Toulouse Street) displays ornamental garden accessories, statuary and fountains made by local artisans. **The Idea Factory** (838 Chartres Street), a delightful place, crafts miniature streetcars, riverboats, Sopwith-Camel planes and all manner of carved items.

RHINO (Canal Place) – the acronym stands for Right Here in New Orleans – is a large gallery showcasing the handiwork of local artisans, including jewelry, decorative items, apparel and paintings.

The Idea Factory

Eating **O**ut

New Orleans boasts of being the only city in the US that has a true regional cuisine. There are definite differences between Cajun food and Creole cuisine, but most local chefs these days say they've merged into "South Louisiana Cooking." (The difference between Cajun and Creole? Creole chefs use rich, rich sauces; Cajun cooking tends to be robust and spicy.) Local menus can be a puzzlement to out-of-towners; here is a food lexicon that may help:

Andouille: a spicy Cajun pork sausage, similar to kielbasa.
Boudin: an even spicier Cajun sausage.
Bananas Foster: a dessert that originated at Brennan's – bananas sautéed in butter, brown sugar, cinnamon and banana liqueur, flamed tableside with white rum and served over vanilla ice cream.
Barbecue shrimp: In the New Orleans version, shrimp are cooked in a garlicky-buttery sauce and served often still encased in their shells. Along with the little critters come plenty of napkins, one or two of which you should use as a bib. This is a very drippy dish.
Beignet: can be a cruller-like pastry (as served at Café du Monde) or a seafood tidbit served as an appetizer.
Café au lait: strong coffee served half-and-half with hot milk; the house drink at Café du Monde.
Chicory: an herb, the roots of which are dried, ground, roasted and used for seasoning coffee.
Crawfish: elsewhere known as crawdads or crayfish, these are like miniature lobsters. They grow in the mud of freshwater streams, and are locally known as mudbugs. Served boiled, or in an étouffée (a spicy sauce that "smothers" the crawfish – *étouffée* is the French for "suffocated").

Crawfish

Dressed: do you want your sandwich dressed? If the answer is yes, that means you want everything on it.
File: ground sassafras leaves, used for seasoning.
Gumbo: a thick soup, always made with rice, and with some com-

Ingredients are the key

bination of okra, file, andouille, chicken or seafood. Gumbo Ya is chicken gumbo.

Jambalaya: a rich mixture of yellow rice, tomatoes, spices, bits of seafood and andouille, tasso, and whatever else you can find in the fridge.

Mirliton: a vegetable pear.

Muffuletta: a huge Italian sandwich, it calls for great slices of bread, Italian meats and cheeses, and a liberal slathering of olive salad. You can order a whole, a half or a quarter; it might be wise to start with a quarter and work up.

Plantain: a cousin of the banana, usually a side dish, fried and simmered in sherry or prepared like candied yams.

Po-boy: New Orleans's answer to the submarine sandwich. Here, they come on crisp slices of French bread.

Praline: a sweet candy patty, made with butter, sugar and pecans.

As a general rule, lunch is served between 11.30am and 2.30 or 3.00pm, dinner from around 7.00pm. Several restaurants have "Early Bird Specials," which means discount dining if you don't mind sitting down at 5.30pm. New Orleans is not a rigidly formal city – the weather has a lot to do with that – but many restaurants do require men to wear a tie and jacket. Some flatly refuse to admit anyone in jeans.

A gratuity is not usually included on the bottom line of the bill, although a few places tack on 15 per cent without advising you of it. As for reservations, it's hard to predict whether or not that'll be necessary. During major events (Mardi Gras, Jazz Fest, big conventions), it'll be tough to get in unless you've reserved far, far in advance. On the other hand, during a slow time you can stroll right into even top-of-the-line restaurants. To be on the safe side, if you're particularly keen on trying a restaurant, make an advance reservation. Note that New Orleans has a steep 9 per cent sales tax. For the following restaurants, the price is based on one meal, exclusive of beverages and tip: over $30 is expensive, under $10 is inexpensive, and in between is moderate.

Po-boy shop

French Quarter

ANTOINE'S
713 St Louis Street
The city's oldest restaurant. Since 1840, chefs here have been creating world-class dishes like Oysters Rockefeller and *pompano en papillote*. The soufflé potatoes are grand. Expensive

ARNAUD'S
813 Bienville Street
A beautiful restaurant, with fine French Creole cuisine and a Sunday jazz brunch. Expensive

Arnaud's

BRENNAN'S
417 Royal Street
Famous for lavish breakfasts with exquisite egg dishes. Expensive

GALATOIRE'S
209 Bourbon Street
French Creole restaurant from 1905. Reservations not accepted. Expensive.

K-PAUL'S LOUISIANA KITCHEN
416 Chartres Street
Home court of world-famous Cajun chef Paul Prudhomme. Expensive

BAYONA
430 Dauphine Street
Serves chef Susan Spicer's New World cuisine. Expensive

MR B'S BISTRO
201 Royal Street
Marvelous seafood, and everything is wonderful from the charcoal grill. Moderate

ALEX PATOUT'S LOUISIANA RESTAURANT
221 Royal Street
Serves authentic South Louisiana cuisine in a lovely setting. Moderate

TUJAGUE'S
823 Decatur Street
The city's second oldest restaurant (1856) is known for excellent boiled brisket of beef and bread pudding (not necessarily together). Moderate

THE ACME OYSTER HOUSE
724 Iberville Street
A very casual place that features raw oysters and ice cold beer. Inexpensive

CROISSANT D'OR
617 Ursuline Street
and its sister
LA MADELEINE
625 Chartres Street
Have the city's best croissants, French pastries and cappuccino. Also croissant sandwiches and quiches. Popular with locals. Inexpensive

CAFÉ DU MONDE
800 Decatur Street
Open around the clock for café au lait and beignets. Locals as well as tourists come here. Inexpensive

THE QUARTER SCENE
900 Dumaine
Has great waffles, sandwiches and salads. Inexpensive

PORT OF CALL
838 Esplanade Avenue
Makes some of the world's best hamburgers. Inexpensive

ST ANN'S DELI
800 Dauphine Street
Eclectic menu includes good chicken, fried steak and juicy BLTs and burgers; they deliver anywhere in the Quarter (call 529-4421). Inexpensive

Central Business District

THE GRILL ROOM
300 Gravier Street
The posh dining room of the Windsor Court Hotel; the menu is a blend of Pacific Rim and American. Expensive

MIKE'S ON THE AVENUE
600 St Charles Avenue
(in the Lafayette Hotel)
Popular for southwestern-cum-American cuisine. Expensive

THE SAZERAC
129 Baronne Street
The plush and romantic dining room of the Fairmont Hotel serves extremely tasty Continental cuisine. Expensive

THE HUMMINGBIRD GRILL
801 St Charles Avenue
A 24-hour greasy spoon with simple fare; not much money goes into interior decorating here. Inexpensive

MOTHER'S
401 Poydras Street
A downscale dive, dishes out memorable breakfasts, red beans and rice, and jambalaya. Inexpensive

Warehouse District

EMERIL'S
800 Tchoupitoulas
Home base of renowned Emeril Lagasse, turns out spicy New American dishes. Everything is homemade here, from andouille to Worcester sauce. Expensive

Garden District

COMMANDER'S PALACE
1403 Washington Avenue
Blends Creole and American cuisines. Wonderful turtle soup; sensational bread pudding soufflé. Expensive

THE CARIBBEAN ROOM
2031 St Charles Avenue
The elegant dining room of the Pontchartrain Hotel serves excellent seafood and steaks. The dessert specialty is Mile High Pie. Expensive

CAFE ATCHAFALAYA
901 Louisiana Avenue

Emeril's

Dishes up good Southern cooking: cornbread, turnip greens, pork chops and suchlike. Moderate

Uptown

GAUTREAU'S
1728 Soniat Street
In a handsome room with pressed tin ceilings, Gautreau's features French Creole cuisine and good steaks. Expensive

UPPERLINE
1413 Upperline Street
The bastion of JoAnne Clevenger, features a "tasting menu," with seven house specialties. Moderate

Nightlife

If you've just landed on the planet, you may not know that New Orleans is the town in which jazz was born. Jelly Roll Morton, who knew a thing or two about tickling the ole ivories, said: "I'm not sure but I think all music was born in New Orleans."

Morton called Buddy Bolden "the blowingest man since Gabriel," and in that he might have been right on. Bolden is the man credited with first playing what came to be called jazz. He was an uptown black, born in 1877, who by the turn of the century had his own band and groupies galore. (Sad to say, there are no existing Bolden recordings, though he did record. Even sadder, at age 30 he was declared "insane," and placed in an institution, where he died 24

Papa's got a brand new bass

years later.) In Buddy's day, his band and others played in clubs over on South Rampart Street, which is why in commemoration there's a giant clarinet painted on the hotel facade of the Holiday Inn Downtown Superdome. The old Funky Butt, Odd Fellows and other jazz halls of Buddy's era are long gone; there's not a trace of them.

Preservation Hall opened in 1961 to try to replicate an old-time jazz hall. The Hall, as it's called, came about as a result of the dedication of Allen Jaffe, a Pennsylvanian tuba player and avid jazz buff. (When Jaffe died in the 1980s, musicians came from all over the world to join one of the biggest jazz funerals the city has ever seen.) Local musicians take busmen's holidays in the Hall, but local civilians wouldn't be caught dead in there. There's no bar and no dancefloor, and besides it's carpeted with tourists.

Though most people think of dixieland or traditional jazz when they think of New Orleans, the real sound of the city is New Orleans funk – a heady mix of R&B and Afro-Caribbean rhythms. Think the Neville Brothers, the Radiators, the Iguanas. Orleanians adore their local heroes, who play around town frequently.

The second most popular music is zydeco, which is the black Creole response to Cajun music. The name "zydeco" springs from the French word for snapbeans: say *les haricots* fast and see what happens. The story goes that while the family musicians practiced on the back porch, the womenfolk were fixin' snapbeans. Thus was born an art form.

There are a few music clubs on Bourbon Street that locals will visit – Maison Bourbon is one, the **Old Absinthe Bar** another – but for the most part the street has been given over to tourists while locals head elsewhere. (There are clubs elsewhere in the French Quarter that are local

Top musicians at Tipitina's

favorites. House of Blues is one that's wildly popular with most people; so is the Dungeon.)

There are some great places uptown, in the university section, and in Riverbend: Muddy Waters (for blues); the Maple Leaf (especially for zydeco); Tipitina's (for a little bit of everything). But if you do go for late-night gamboling "out there," as Quarterites call anything outside their beloved Quarter, call for a cab to bring you back. (To put it in the vernacular, "Don't get excited, call United." United Cab, tel: 522-7721.) If you want to go hog-wild, or at least first-class, call London Livery to reserve a limo for the night (tel: 831-0700).

If you opt to hang on Bourbon, know the rules of the road. Most places have a two-drink minimum per set, and sets last about 15 or 20 minutes. In some cases you're required to take both drinks at once. Don't argue with the bouncers. Remember, some clip joints can be wildly fun, if you happen to be on an expense account and money is no obstacle. Note, too, that some house drink prices can be mighty mysterious. Cover charges range from $5 to $20, depending on the venue.

And speaking of drinks, New Orleans bartenders turn out some potent concoctions. Matter of fact, New Orleans claims to have created the first cocktail. According to local legend, in the early 1800s a French chemist named Antoine Amedée Peychaud had an apothecary shop on Royal Street. For customers who complained of digestive distress, Peychaud prescribed his "bitters," which he served in an egg-cup. The French word for such a cup is *coquetier*, and faster than you can say "Sazerac," the Americans turned the word into "cocktail." Peychaud's stomach remedy was made with his own bitters, Sazerac-de-Forge cognac and absinthe. Absinthe has long been illegal – New Orleanian bartenders substitute for it the locally made Herbsaint – and rye whiskey usually pinch-hits for Sazerac. The only original ingredient is

Sax appeal

78

Peychaud bitters. Be that as it may, that Sazerac cocktail is the house drink at the Fairmont's Sazerac Bar.

The ubiquitous Hurricane originated at Pat O'Brien's in the 1930s. Pat's partner, Charlie Cantrell, let an aggressive drummer sell him 60 bottles of rum. For good measure, the salesman tossed in some glasses shaped like hurricane lamps. In an effort to get that rum moving, Cantrell told the bartenders to mix in some passion fruit, serve it in the hurricane glasses, and tout it as the house drink. An historic moment. The Ramos gin fizz, the local version of a gin fizz, blends gin, orange-flower water, egg whites, and soda.

Like Las Vegas, New Orleans is a 24-hour town, which means there's no legal closing time. A few bars never close; some close at midnight; one or two don't open till midnight. Best to call before going bar-hopping at two or three in the morning. (Going bar-hopping at two or three in the morning is not unusual here.)

Music is not limited to dry land. Jazz goes rolling on the river, too, on the steamboat *Natchez* (tel: 586-8777) and the *Creole Queen* (tel: 524-0814). Both boats have dixieland bands, plunkety-plunk banjos, and buffets that feature regional cuisine. And besides all that, you'll have the mighty Mississippi, the world's most romantic river, right under your feet.

To find out who's doing what where, *Offbeat*, a free newspaper devoted to the local music scene, can be found in bookstores and on newsstands, as can *Gambit*, a free weekly newspaper that has a great calendar of events. So does *Lagniappe*, a tabloid section in the Friday *Times-Picayune*. *Where* and *This Week in New Orleans*, both of which are distributed free to hotels, also have news about music clubs and events.

Music clubs in the French Quarter

It may be touristy, and uncomfortable to boot (crowded, seedy, and you may have to stand), but **Preservation Hall** should not be missed. Traditional jazz as played by legends of the genre. Gates open at 7.30, music stomps off at 8.00, closes at midnight. 726 St Peter Street, tel: (night) 523-8939, (day) 522-2841.

The **Palm Court Jazz Café** features traditional or dixieland Thursday-Sunday, R&B Wednesday. 1204 Decatur Street, tel: 525-0200.

The House of Blues is a huge place crowded with enthusiastic fans; good food. 225 Decatur Street, tel: 529-2624.

The **Old Absinthe Bar** is another bluesy place, best very late at night. 400 Bourbon Street, tel: 525-8108.

The **Cajun Cabin** sends the sounds of Cajun music way out into the street, and serves good Cajun food, too. 504 Bourbon Street, tel: 529-4256.

Locals turn out at **Maison Bourbon** to catch Wallace Davenport and Tommy Yetta. 641 Bourbon Street, tel: 522-8818.

Donna's Bar & Grill, on the cusp of the Quarter, features brass bands. 800 N. Rampart Street, tel: 596-6914.

The Famous Door, a touristy place since 1934, does traditional jazz, some R&B; a mixed bag, really. 339 Bourbon Street, tel: 522-7623.

Snug Harbor is popular with Orleanians, mainly for the great local entertainers. 626 Frenchmen Street, tel: 949-0696.

Harbor from the storm

Margaritaville is the local branch of Jimmy Buffet's Key West Club, replete with jazz and Cheeseburgers in Paradise. 1104 Decatur Street, tel: 592-2565.

Young people tend to hang out in droves at the **Hard Rock Café**. 440 N. Peter Street, tel: 529-5617.

Maxwell's caters to tourists with dixieland and traditional jazz. 615 Toulouse Street, tel: 523-4207.

Chris Owens' Club is a supper club in which Ms Owens does a classy Las Vegas-style revue. 500 Bourbon Street, tel: 523-6400.

The accents and sounds are very Irish at **O'Flaherty's Irish Channel**, where the Celtic Folk play and headliners like Tommy Makem sometimes put in appearances. 508 Toulouse Street, tel: 529-1317.

Pat O'Brien's, a veritable institution, has three bars and goes strong till the wee small hours. 718 St Peter Street, tel: 525-4823.

Rhythms has a huge dance floor and bluesy music nightly. 227 Bourbon Street, tel: 523-3800.

In a class by itself, the **Dungeon**, a grungy place beloved of visiting celebs, has no phone and no discernible address. Roughly 736 Toulouse Street, next to the Tropical Isle.

And when all is said and done, the Esplanade Lounge in the lobby of the **Royal Orleans** is a great place for unwinding. 621 St Louis Street, tel: 529-5333.

The **Napoleon House** (500 Chartres Street, tel: 524-9752) and **Lafitte's Blacksmith Shop** (941 Bourbon Street, tel: 523-0066) are both time-honored institutions of higher imbibing.

Out There

Rock-N-Bowl

One of the hottest spots is town is the 1940s-era **Mid-City Bowling Lanes Rock-N-Bowl**, with live zydeco and a dance floor next to the lanes. 4133 S. Carrollton Avenue, tel: 482-3133.

Cavernous **Tipitina's** is a veritable shrine to New Orleans music. 501 Napoleon Avenue, tel: 895-8477 (concert line: 897-3943).

Home court of clarinettist Pete Fountain, one of the city's favorite sons, is the eponymous **Pete Fountain's Club**, on the third floor of the Hilton Riverside Hotel. 2 Poydras Street, tel: 523-4374.

In the atrium of the luxury **Le Meridien Hotel**, sophisticated jazz is played every night. 614 Canal Street, tel: 525-6500.

Jimmy's Club is where the college crowd heads to hear good rock. 8200 Willow Street, Uptown, tel: 861-8200.

Everyone who loves blues turns up at **Muddy Waters**, 8301 Oak Street, Uptown, tel: 866-7174.

Across the street from Muddy Waters, the **Maple Leaf** draws all ages for zydeco, Cajun, R&B, whatever. 8316 Oak Street, Uptown, tel: 866-9359.

Cooter Brown's is a downscale college hang-out with pool tables, loud taped music, and more brands of beer than you ever heard of. 509 S. Carrollton Avenue, tel: 866-9104.

There's a good dance floor and Cajun dance lessons at **Michaul's Live Cajun Music Restaurant**, 840 St Charles Avenue, Warehouse District, tel: 522-5517.

There's more Cajun food and dancing to live music at **Mulate's**, 201 Julia Street, Warehouse District, tel: 522-1492.

Go for gospel to the Praline Connection

Traditional jazz and soul food are the fare at the **Praline Connection Gospel & Blues Hall**, 907 St Peter Street, tel: 523-3973.

Casinos

Gambling in Louisiana has had a hard row to hoe. In 1991, the state legislature approved a single land-based casino for New Orleans and 15 gambling riverboats for the state's waterways. Since that time, Harrah's New Orleans, which was tapped to operate the land-based casino, has gone bankrupt, some water-based casinos have refused to leave the dock, which the law required them to do, and riverboat casinos have been paddling around from river to river, lake to lake all over the state like latter-day Flying Dutchmen. At press time, three riverboat casinos were operating in the New Orleans area. All of them are dressed to the nines in fine 19th-century style, all are aslosh with one-armed bandits, gaming tables, entertainment and food. And drink, of course.

The most successful such enterprise is the **Treasure Chest** which docks on Lake Ponchartrain in Kenner, across from the Pontchartrain Center (5050 Williams Boulevard, Kenner, tel: 443-8000 or 800-298-0711). The **Belle of Orleans** is also on Lake Pontchartrain but to the east, adjacent to the Lakefront Airport (1 Stars & Stripes Boulevard, tel: 248-3200 or 800-572-2559). And the **Boomtown Belle Casino**, done up in a Wild-West motif, is on the Harvey Canal on the west bank (4132 Peters Road, tel: 366-7711 or 800-366-7711).

At press time, the **Flamingo** (tel: 587-7777 or, outside New Orleans, tel: 800-587-5825), docked at the Poydras Street Wharf behind the Hilton Hotel, was scheduled to depart for the Red River in Shreveport. But as anyone knows who's observed the gambling scene in New Orleans, there's many a slip 'twixt the cup and the lip. When you arrive, the Flamingo may well still be here.

The Arts

Touring companies of Broadway shows tread the boards at the 2,000-seat **Saenger Performing Arts Centre theatre**. 143 N. Rampart Street, CBD, tel: 524-2490.

Top-name entertainers perform at the **Kiefer UNO Lakefront Arena**, (6801 Franklin Avenue, Lakefront, tel: 286-7222) or in the **Louisiana Superdome** (1500 Poydras Street, CBD, tel: 587-3800). For tickets for performances at those venues, call Ticketmaster (522-5555). New Orleans's only Equity theater is the **Southern Repertory Theater**, whose productions are mounted in their own theater on the third level of Canal Place (tel: 861-8163).

Le Petit Théâtre du Vieux Carré is one of the nation's oldest continuously performing community theaters. Le Petit, in a lovely building at 616 St Peter Street at Jackson Square, does a season of seven or eight plays and musicals beginning in September (tel: 522-2081 for details).

The **Contemporary Arts Center** in the Warehouse District presents avant-garde theater in their two theaters. 900 Camp Street, tel: 523-1216.

The Louisiana Philharmonic Orchestra performs a season of classical music and pops at the **Orpheum Theatre**. 129 University Place, tel: 524-3285.

New Orleans has neither a resident opera company nor a resident ballet company. Both the **New Orleans Ballet Association** (tel: 522-0996) and the **New Orleans Opera Association** (tel: 529-2278) are producing entities that bring touring companies to perform in New Orleans. Ballet and opera are performed at the **Theatre for the Performing Arts** in Armstrong Park.

Good theater at the Saenger

Calendar of Special Events

JANUARY/FEBRUARY

The new year begins with a double whammy. The annual **Sugar Bowl** game (a college football contest) is played in the Louisiana Superdome either New Year's Eve or New Year's Day, with all the attendant hoopla both inside and all around the Superdome.

A very noisy **New Year's Eve Countdown** explodes in Jackson Square and environs, replete with fireworks and yelling. Before the dust settles the **Carnival** season kicks off on January 6 (Twelfth Night), beginning a roughly two-month partying period that gradually crescendos and culminates with two weeks of **Mardi Gras** frenzy, and comes to a screeching halt at midnight Ash Wednesday. (The date of Mardi Gras varies, depending upon when Easter falls.)

Another January event is the week-long **New Orleans Film and Video Festival**, screening the best foreign and domestic films.

MARCH

A full calendar in March opens with the **Black Heritage Festival**, featuring soul food, gospel and the blues, followed by **parades** honoring St Patrick and St Joseph, and two very popular literary events, notably the **Tennessee Williams/New Orleans Literary Festival** and the **Faulkner Festival**.

APRIL/MAY

On the Friday after Easter (a lovely time to visit), the **Spring Fiesta** begins with a carriage parade through the Quarter. Many private homes are open for tours.

In early April, the **French Quarter**

French Quarter carriages, springtime

Jazz Fest, late April and early May

Festival transforms the Vieux Carré into a huge block party, with plenty of music and food.

For locals, the favored fest is the New Orleans Jazz & Heritage Festival, better known as **Jazz Fest**, an internationally acclaimed celebration of the city's famed food, music and crafts. Attracting people from all over the world, it begins the last weekend in April and extends through the first weekend in May.

Some of the top names in the music business make their way to the city at this time, to play either in the Fair Grounds near City Park where the festival itself takes place, or in a variety of venues around town.

JUNE/JULY

In June, there is yet more music and food during the **Great French Market Tomato Festival**, and in July, Independence Day is celebrated with entertainment, food and sizzling fireworks displays at the day-long **Go 4th on the River**.

Later in July, the city's best chefs and beverage managers contribute their talents and products for a weekend of wine-tastings during the **New Orleans Food & Wine Experience**.

SEPTEMBER/OCTOBER

In September, the **African Heritage Festival International** brings entertainment and food to Armstrong Park.

In October, the **Swamp Festival** salutes the Cajun culture at Audubon Zoo, while the **Carnaval Latino** devotes four heady days to celebrations of the Latin culture.

NOVEMBER/DECEMBER

Beginning in late November, City Park's majestic trees sparkle with hundreds of lights for the month-long **Celebration in the Oaks**. It's a time when the park, often overlooked by tourists who think New Orleans is only the French Quarter, comes into its own. Then all through December **A New Orleans Christmas** means parades, caroling and parties.

In Cajun river parishes just west of New Orleans, **Bonfires on the Levee** is an ages-old tradition of building giant bonfires and torching them on Christmas Eve, to light the way for Papa Noel, the Cajun Santa Claus.

And in the wink of an eye it's time to start all over, with the Sugar Bowl, the Countdown, and Carnival!

Practical Information

Unless otherwise noted, all telephone numbers are preceded by the area code (504).

By Air: New Orleans is served by all major US carriers (American, Delta, Continental, Northwest, Southwest, TWA, US Air), as well as by AeroMexico, British Airways, Sasha, Taca and charters. Air travelers put down at New Orleans International Airport, also called Moisant Field, (tel: 464-0831) about 15 miles (24km) west of the city in the town of Kenner. The much smaller Lakefront Airport in eastern New Orleans is for private and corporate planes.

By Water: The mighty Mississippi River is far and away the most scenic route to the

American Queen

city. The historic *Delta Queen* and her two larger siblings, the *Mississippi Queen* and the *American Queen*, ply the waters between New Orleans and ports as far

north as St Paul, Minnesota, stopping at river cities all along the way. Dressed in elegant 19th-century style, the boats make two- to 12-night cruises, replete with rousing entertainment and relaxing, deck rocking chairs.

Several theme cruises (Big Band, Fall Foliage, the Good Old Summertime) are offered during the year. Somewhat pricey, the cruises target well-heeled retired folk, with whom they are enormously popular. Details from a travel agent or the Delta Queen Steamboat Company, 30 Robin Street Wharf, New Orleans, LA 70130, tel: (toll-free) 1-800-543-1949.

The nation's first luxury river barge also casts off from homeport New Orleans. Comprising two river barges propelled by a 3,000-horsepower towboat, the *River Explorer* is a two-deck, 200-passenger floating resort hotel which travels the country's rivers and inland waterways at a pace far removed from modern travel.

Three- to nine-night excursions focus on the food, music and history of cultures as diverse as the Amish and the Cajuns. (Motorcoach shore excursions are included in the fare.) On-barge amenities include a two-story theater, cabaret and entertainment complex, bars and lounges, walking and jogging track, and barbecue grills. Each stateroom has a minibar, a satellite TV and VCR, a telephone, a large bath and picture windows. Contact RiverBarge Excursion Lines, 201 Opelousas Avenue, New Orleans, LA 70114, tel: 365-0022.

By Rail: Amtrak trains connect New Orleans with Los Angeles, Miami, Chicago,

New York and Washington, DC, among other cities. The arrival and departure point is the Union Passenger Terminal in the Central Business District. For information, call Amtrak, tel: (toll-free) 1-800-USA-RAIL.

By Bus: Union Passenger Terminal is also the arrival and departure point for Greyhound buses (tel: toll-free 1-800-231-2222), whose routes criss-cross the continental US from coast to coast.

By Road: For automobile travelers, the main east-west artery through the city is Interstate-10 (I-10), which strings across the southern US, including downtown New Orleans, from Miami to Los Angeles. Interstate-55 (I-55) is a north-south route which connects with I-10 just west of New Orleans.

Other major routes through town are US 90 and US 61 (also called Airline Highway). To drive in Louisiana, you must have a valid driving license (an international license is not required), a vehicle-registration document and proof of automobile insurance. Non-citizens must also have a valid passport.

TRAVEL ESSENTIALS

Visas and Passports

A valid passport is required for citizens of Great Britain and Canada who are visiting the US for up to 90 days and who have a return ticket. Citizens of most other countries must have a valid passport, a visa and a return or ongoing ticket. Regulations at city gateways vary regarding transit stops, and a visa may be required for re-entry after a visit outside the US. Vaccinations are not required for entry into the US.

Climate

Average daily high and low temperatures for New Orleans:

Month	High	Low
January	17C (62F)	8C (47F)
February	18C (65F)	10C (50F)
March	22C (71F)	13C (55F)
April	25C (77F)	16C (61F)
May	28C (83F)	20C (68F)
June	31C (88F)	23C (73C)
July	32C (90F)	23C (74F)
August	32C (90F)	24C (76F)
September	30C (86F)	24C (76F)
October	26C (79F)	18C (64F)
November	21C (70F)	13C (55F)
December	18C (64F)	9C (48F)

When to Visit

Spring and fall are fine times to visit New Orleans. By mid-April, the city has blossomed in subtropical finery, temperatures are moderate and the humidity is bearable. The same conditions usually prevail in October. Do not plan a first visit during Mardi Gras. Everyone should see "The Greatest Free Show on Earth" at least once, but during Mardi Gras the city's charms are virtually obliterated, buried beneath hordes of merrymakers.

In June, July and August, hotel rates plummet as the temperature and humidity soar, and the daily forecast is, "Highs in the nineties with possibility of scattered afternoon thundershowers."

Clothing

When locals "dress up," they dress to the nines. But for streetwear, particularly in the French Quarter, with its armies of tourists, you'd almost think there was a dress code insisting on teeshirts, jeans and sneakers. (In warm weather – nine months of the year – the "code" is relaxed to allow halter tops, short-shorts and even rubber flip-flops.)

The city's high-end restaurants do require "proper attire." In some of them jeans are verboten, and many require jacket and tie for men. Bring cottons for summer, lightweight woolens for winter. Also

All dressed up

in winter, rely on "layering." You'll be glad you brought your umbrella and that all-weather coat with zip-out lining.

MONEY MATTERS

American visitors: Most, but not all hotels, restaurants and shops accept major credit cards (American Express, Diners Club, MasterCard and Visa). Do not carry large amounts of cash; do not get cash from an Automatic Teller Machine (ATM) on a dark deserted street. Travelers checks are widely accepted, though you may need proof of identification when cashing the checks at a bank.

Overseas visitors: The best rates of exchange are at banks, which are open weekdays from 9am till 3 or 4pm. Bring your passports. There is a foreign currency exchange at the Whitney Bank in the Central Business District (228 St Charles Avenue, tel: 586-7272) and at the airport (tel: 838-6490). Whitney Bank and First NBC are among bank branches in the French Quarter; their main offices are in the Central Business District, along with many others. There is also an exchange at the airport Business Center (tel: 465-9647).

ATMs are sprinkled throughout the metropolitan area. For US Plus locations, tel: 1-800-843-7587; for Cirrus, 1-800-424-7787.

Louisiana Tax-Free Shopping: Overseas visitors can take advantage of the state's unique tax-free shopping plan. It works this way: look for shops, hotels, and restaurants that display the LTFS insignia. Pay full price for your purchase, including the 9 per cent sales tax, and get a voucher for the tax. Upon departure, visit the Louisiana Tax-Free Shopping offices at the airport, present your passport, return airline ticket and voucher to claim a sales tax rebate. Amounts up to $500 will be refunded on the spot; amounts over $500 will be sent to your home address.

GETTING AROUND

Airport Connections

The Airport Shuttle (tel: 522-3500), which boards just outside the baggage claim area, operates around the clock, dropping off passengers at area hotels. The trip can take anywhere from 20 minutes to an hour. One-way fare is around $10; a reservation is required for the return trip.

Public buses of Louisiana Transit (tel: 737-9611) operate between the CBD (Elk Place at Tulane Avenue) and the airport. The fare is cheap for the 45-minute trip.

Taxis offer the fastest service into town (20 to 30 minutes, depending on traffic). The set fare is under $25 for one or two people, plus extra for each additional passenger. The most reliable taxi company is United (tel: 522-7711, toll-free 1-800-323-3303); you can arrange in advance of your arrival for a cab to pick you up at the airport. Other steadfast radio taxis are Yellow-Checker Cabs (943-2411) and Liberty Bell Cabs (822-5974).

Taxis, Streetcars and Buses

The French Quarter is best seen on foot at a leisurely gait, and much of the Central Business District (CBD) and the Garden District are easily walkable. Taxis can usually be hailed in the CBD and the Quarter, but they don't often cruise elsewhere.

There is a fixed charge to begin, with

Making tracks

extra charges for each additional passenger and a rise in price every 40 seconds. For special events like Mardi Gras, more charges are added. For complaints call the Taxi Commission (tel: 565-6572).

Streetcars and buses are operated by

the Regional Transit Authority (RTA, tel: 248-3900). The fare is the same for buses and the St Charles streetcar, a little more for the Riverfront streetcar. The RTA also operates the French Quarter shuttle, which looks like a miniature streetcar running between the Quarter and the CBD.

A Visitour pass, available in hotels and

shopping malls, allows unlimited riding on buses and streetcars; prices are for one day or four days.

Driving

"Big Easy" does not really describe driving conditions in New Orleans. It can be maddening. The Quarter is small, often crowded, and laced with one-way streets. Assuming you could actually find a parking place, parking rules favor Quarter residents and the signs are indecipherable. Meter maids and tow-truck operators are swift and unmerciful. (The Claiborne Auto Pound is at 400 N. Claiborne Avenue, tel: 565-7450.)

Street signs downtown (the CBD and French Quarter) are easily read; in other areas they are not even easily found. Don't even think about driving around town during Mardi Gras. However unwittingly you block a parade route, your car will be hauled away and it'll cost $100 to get it back. It's best to put your car in a se-

cured place and leave it until you need it for excursions.

Rental cars are available at Avis (tel: 1-800-331-1212), Budget (1-800-527-0700), Dollar (1-800-800-4000) and Hertz (1-800-654-3131).

HOURS AND HOLIDAYS

Official Holidays

January 1 **New Year's Day**
January 18 **Martin Luther King Day**
February **President's Day**
February or March **Mardi Gras Day**
March or April **Good Friday** and **Easter**
Last Monday in May **Memorial Day**
July 4 **Independence Day**
First Monday in September **Labor Day**
November 1 **All Saints' Day**
Last Thursday in November **Thanksgiving**
December 25 **Christmas Day**

Opening Times

Office hours city-wide are usually Monday through Friday 9 till 5. The main Post Office (701 Loyola Avenue) is open Monday-Friday 8.30am till 4.30pm, Saturday 8.30am till noon. Most CBD and French Quarter shops are open Monday through Saturday from 9.30 or 10am until 5 or 6pm, Sunday noon till 5pm. Closing time in the Quarter can be whimsical, depending upon the number of tourists in town.

Mall hours are more reliable. The Jax Brewery is open Sunday through Thursday 10am till 9pm, Friday and Saturday 10am till 10pm. The Canal Place mall is open daily 10am till midnight, but most shops close at 6pm. New Orleans Centre shops are open Monday through Saturday 10am till 8pm, Sunday till 6. The Riverwalk mall is open Monday through Saturday 10am till 9pm, Sunday 11 till 7.

Hours for museums and art galleries vary greatly; it's best to call ahead.

ACCOMMODATION

Most people prefer to stay in the French Quarter, which has lodgings from the deluxe to the quaint, with many of the latter in 19th-century Creole townhouses. Thanks to a years-long moratorium on building in the Quarter, all of the new hotels are in the CBD. Largely catering to conventioneers, most are luxurious high-rises, replete with health clubs, razzle-dazzle entertainment and state-of-the-art technological wizardry.

Garden District hotels are for those who prefer a quiet, genteel neighborhood; it's five minutes from downtown via the St Charles Streetcar. As in most large cities, the airport area is awash with hotels and motels geared toward business travelers.

In recent years, bed-and-breakfast inns have cropped up all over town – as they have all over the country. Here, as elsewhere, the term "bed-and-breakfast" is quite elastic, and can mean anything from a room in a modest home to a deluxe cabin aboard the *Delta Queen* steamboat.

Unlike, say, the Caribbean, New Orleans has no specific high and low seasons. "High" season is any time the city is inundated with visitors, be it Mardi Gras or during a major convention. Up until a few years ago, the Crescent City was a veritable ghost town during the hot-stickety summer months. However, thanks to the yeoman work of the Tourist Commission, huge conventions are pouring in as often in July as in November.

Hotel rates depend entirely upon the number of tourists in the city. When you call to request rates, the reservations clerk will first ask what dates you plan to be in town. (Many hotels do not even publish a rate sheet.)

For Mardi Gras, hotel rates can triple and a four- or five-day minimum is often required, sometimes payable in advance, in full. When you reserve a room, especially for a major event, be sure to ask what the cancellation policy is. (Expect utter chaos during Mardi Gras. New Orleans wrote the book on crowd control, but Mardi Gras revelers tend to be, ummm, unruly.)

In the following list, the price codes refer to a standard double room with private bath:

$ = up to $95
$$ = $95-125
$$$ = $125-150
$$$$ over $150

The French Quarter

THE CLAIBORNE MANSION
2111 Dauphine Street
Tel: 949-7327
On the fringe of the Quarter in Faubourg Marigny, this posh, secluded bed-and-breakfast has spacious rooms, four-poster and canopied beds, a lush courtyard with pool, voice mail and VCRs. $$$$

OMNI ROYAL ORLEANS HOTEL
621 St Louis Street
Tel: 529-5333
The Royal O, in the center of the Quarter, has a stunning white marble lobby, average-sized rooms with marble baths, and a rooftop pool. The popular Rib Room restaurant is here. $$$$

Carousel bar at the Monteleone

MONTELEONE HOTEL
214 Royal Street
Tel: 523-3341
If the Monteleone were a woman, she would be an elegant dowager empress. Built in 1886, in a great location two blocks from the CBD, it has 600 luxurious rooms and suites, restaurants and rooftop pool. $$$

DAUPHINE ORLEANS
415 Dauphine Street
Tel: 586-1800

Four blocks from Canal Street, one block from Bourbon; 111 rooms with minibars, complimentary Continental breakfast. Pool, exercise room, outdoor hot tub. $$$

Le Richelieu

Le Richelieu
1234 Chartres Street
Tel: 529-2492
One of the city's best bargains offers individually decorated rooms with slow-moving ceiling fans, many with balconies and mirrored walls, a restaurant, lounge, and pool. $$

Hotel Villa Convento
616 Ursulines Street
Tel: 522-1793
Small, cozy and friendly, the 25-room family owned and operated guest house is near the Old Ursuline Convent. No pool, but Continental breakfast (included) is served in a tree-shaded courtyard. $

Central Business District

Fairmont
University Place
Tel: 529-7111
Built in 1893 and fully refurbished in 1997, this is everybody's idea of a grand hotel. Spacious rooms, suites with fax machines, the romantic Sazerac restaurant, and a fine fitness center. One block from the Quarter. $$$$

Windsor Court Hotel
300 Gravier Street
Tel: 523-6000
The city's most luxurious hotel receives numerous awards for both the hotel and the Grill Room restaurant. The balconied high rise is at the foot of Canal Street, across from Canal Place. $$$$

Courtyard by Marriott
124 St Charles Avenue
Tel: 581-9005
A superb Mardi Gras location, this chain hotel built in 1995 has spacious rooms, cable TV with movie channels, phones with dataports, an exercise room, indoor pool, hot tub and restaurant. Convenient to the Quarter and shops. $$$$

Hampton Inn
226 Carondelet Street
Tel: 529-9990
A boon for budget travelers, two blocks from Bourbon Street, this 186-room hotel provides complimentary Continental breakfast, free local calls, hair dryers and an exercise room. $$

Warehouse District

Embassy Suites Hotel
315 Julia Street
Tel: 525-1993
This all-suites property is convenient to the Convention Center and art galleries. Each two-room suite has a kitchenette with microwave and coffeemaker, and phones with voice mail and dataport. Full breakfast included in the rate. Outdoor pool, Jacuzzi and exercise room. $$$$

Holiday Inn Select
881 Convention Center Boulevard
Tel: 524-1881
Across from the Convention Center, this hotel caters to business travelers: rooms have desks with good lighting, phones with dataports and voice mail, bath phones. Complimentary Continental breakfast. $$

Garden District

Pontchartrain Hotel
2031 St Charles Avenue
Tel: 524-0581
Stately and sedate, the Pontchartrain celebrated its 70th birthday in 1997. Accommodations range from small pension rooms in the rear to some of the

city's most sumptuous suites. Home of the fine Caribbean Room restaurant. $$$$

SULLY MANSION
2631 Prytania Street
Tel: 891-0457
A handsome Queen Anne house, this is a bed-and-breakfast one block from the St Charles Streetcar. Each room has a private bath and phone. $$

ST CHARLES GUEST HOUSE
1748 Prytania Street
Tel: 523-6556
A favorite of backpackers and budget travelers, the St Charles has modest accommodations, pool and complimentary Continental breakfast. Near the Garden District, one block off St Charles streetcar line. $

Mid-City

HOSTELLING INTERNATIONAL
2253 Carondelet Street
Tel: 523-3014
One block from the streetcar, this large hostel has dormitory rooms with bunk beds, private rooms with shared baths and full apartments. Two communal kitchens. $

HEALTH & EMERGENCIES

Many hospitals in town have 24-hour emergency rooms. The two nearest the French Quarter are Tulane University Medical Center (1415 Tulane Avenue, tel: 588-5268) and the Medical Center of Louisiana, which locals call Charity Hospital (1532 Tulane Avenue, tel: 568-

2311). Touro Infirmary (1401 Foucher, tel: 897-7011) serves the Garden District and Uptown.

The French Quarter's only pharmacy, Royal Pharmacy (1101 Royal Street, tel: 523-5401) is open Monday through Saturday 10am till 6pm. There are 24-hour pharmacies at Eckerd (3400 Canal Street, tel: 488-6661) and at two Walgreen Drug Stores (3057 Gentilly Boulevard, tel: 282-2621; 3311 Canal Street, tel: 822-8070). There are Walgreen stores at 900 Canal Street and at Royal and Iberville streets in the Quarter, but neither one of these has a pharmacy.

To locate a dentist, call the Dental Information Service (tel: 522-2206) and leave a message.

As in any other major tourist destination, pickpockets prey on brashly obvious tourists, especially during Mardi Gras. Don't carry large amounts of cash, and pay attention to your wallet or purse. Unattractive though they may be, money belts are much safer. Don't leave money, your passport or jewelry in your hotel room. Put your valuables in the hotel safety deposit vault.

New Orleans is not a good place to wander around exploring. Avoid walking down dark, deserted streets anywhere in town. Safe neighborhoods are often cheek by jowl with unsavory ones, and the borders are almost impossible to distinguish. The French Quarter is safe for walking around during the day, but at night stay near the crowds. Avoid Rampart Street at night, and do not go into Armstrong Park except with large crowds to attend opera or ballet performances.

After hours in the French Quarter

Useful Numbers

Emergency (Police, Fire, Ambulance) 911
Police (non-emergency) 821-2222
Post Office US Postal Service 24-hour recorded information: 1-800-725-2161
  Main Branch
  (701 Poydras Street) 589-1111
  Vieux Carré
  (1022 Iberville Street) 524-0072
Regional Transit Authority Lost and Found (2619 Canal Street) 569-2625
AIDS Hotline 524-2437
Telephone Directory Assistance 1-411

COMMUNICATIONS & MEDIA

Telephones

Almost all hotels and guest houses provide private phones for guests; however most also levy a surcharge, even for credit call cards. Pay phones can be found on the streets, in the lobby of most hotels and large office buildings, and in shopping malls, bars and restaurants. Almost all public telephones have been converted from dial to button. Lift the receiver, deposit coins (25¢) and listen for the dial tone, then touch the desired number. There is no charge for 911 emergency calls.

Clowning around

To dial other countries, dial 011, then the country and then the city code. The country code for the United Kingdom is 44; for Italy, 39; for Germany, 49; for Australia, 61; for France, 33; for Greece, 30; for Israel, 972; for Japan, 81.

Postal Service

The main branch of the US Postal Service is at 701 Poydras Street in the CBD. For 24-hour recorded information, call 800-725-2161. The main Post Office is open Monday through Friday 8.30am to 4.30pm, Saturday 8.30am till noon. Window C at the main branch is open 24 hours a day. The Vieux Carré (French Quarter) branch is at 1022 Iberville Street, open the same hours as the main Post Office. The French Quarter Postal Emporium (940 Royal Street, tel: 525-6651) is a private service, not affiliated to the US Postal Service. In addition to most services of the official Post Office (at somewhat higher prices), they also provide fax and photocopying services.

What's On

Publications with calendars of local events include *Lagniappe*, a tabloid section in the Friday edition of the *Times-Picayune*; *Gambit*, a free weekly newspaper of local news and reviews found in bookstores, newsstands and some supermarkets; *Where* and *This Week in New Orleans*, both distributed free to area hotels.

USEFUL ADDRESSES

Tourist Information

Before arriving, write for information to the New Orleans Metropolitan Convention & Visitors Bureau, 1520 Sugar Bowl Drive, tel: 566-5011 or 800-672-6124. Once you're there, the best walk-in services are the New Orleans Welcome Center, 529 St Ann Street in Jackson Square, and in the same building the Louisiana Office of Tourism. Both entities have free maps, brochures and friendly advice about New Orleans and environs.

Consulates

Argentina World Trade Center
tel: 523-2823
Austria 755 Magazine Street
tel: 581-5141
Bangladesh 321 St Charles Avenue
tel: 581-1979
Barbados 321 St Charles Avenue
Tel: 586-1979
Belgium 611 Gravier Street

Tel: 522-3591
Belize 520 Gravier Street
Tel: 523-7750
Brazil 650 Poydras Street
Tel: 588-9178
Chile 2 Canal Street
Tel: 523-4368
Colombia 2 Canal Street
Tel: 525-5580
Costa Rica 2002 20th Street, Kenner
Tel: 468-3948
Denmark 321 St Charles Avenue
Tel: 586-5300
Dominican Republic 2 Canal Street
Tel: 522-1843
Ecuador 2 Canal Street
Tel: 523-3229
El Salvador 2 Canal Street
Tel: 522-4266
Finland 1100 Poydras Street
Tel: 523-6451
France 3305 St Charles Avenue
Tel: 897-6387
Germany 225 Baronne Street
Tel: 569-4289
Greece 2 Canal Street
Tel: 523-1167
Guatemala 2 Canal Street
Tel: 525-0013
Haiti 611 Gravier Street
Tel: 586-8309
Honduras 203 Carondelet Street
Tel: 522-3118
India 201 St Charles Avenue
Tel: 582-8000
Italy 630 Camp Street
Tel: 524-2271
Japan One Poydras Plaza
Tel: 529-2101
Korea 321 St Charles Avenue
Tel: 586-1979
Liberia 333 St Charles Avenue
Tel: 523-5300
Luxembourg 8012 Oak Street
Tel: 861-3743
Mexico World Trade Center
Tel: 522-3596
Netherlands 643 Magazine Street
Tel: 596-2838
Panama 2 Canal Street
Tel: 525-3458
Peru 611 Gravier Street
Tel: 525-2706
Philippines 2 Canal Street

Tel: 525-5225
Portugal 509 N. Carrollton Avenue
Tel: 482-4115
Spain World Trade Center
Tel: 525-4951
Sweden 2640 Canal Street
Tel: 827-8600
Switzerland 1620 Eighth Street
Tel: 897-6510
Thailand 335 Julia Street
Tel: 522-3400
United Kingdom 321 St Charles Avenue
Tel: 524-4180
Uruguay 2 Canal Street
Tel: 525-8354
Venezuela 2 Canal Street
Tel: 522-3284

FURTHER READING

A Confederacy of Dunces by John Kennedy
Toole. Grove Press, New York 1980.
*Beautiful Crescent: A History of New
Orleans* by Joan B. Garvey and Mary Lou
Widmer. Garmer Press 1982.
*Haunted City: An Unauthorized Guide to
the Magical Magnificent New Orleans of
Anne Rice* by Joy Dickinson. Carol
Publishing Group 1995.
Insight Guide: New Orleans Edited by
Martha Ellen Zenfell Apa Publications
1997.
Interview with the Vampire by Anne Rice.
Knopf 1976.
The Moviegoer by Walker Percy. Avon
1961.
Old Creole Days by George Washington
Cable. Scribner's 1916.
Vampire Lestat by Anne Rice. Knopf 1990.
Voodoo in New Orleans by Robert Tallant.
Pelican 1983.
The Witching Hour,
another by local Anne
Rice. Knopf 1990.

ACKNOWLEDGMENTS

*The author would like to thank Beverly Gianna at the Greater New Orleans
Tourist & Convention Commission*

Photography Alex Demyan
Production Editor Mohammed Dar
Handwriting V Barl
Cover Design Klaus Geisler
Cartography Berndtson & Berndtson